A PLEASUR

A PLEASURE OF GARDENS

A LITERARY COMPANION

Edited by
Joyce and Maurice Lindsay

Drawings by
Morven Cameron

ABERDEEN UNIVERSITY PRESS
Member of Maxwell Macmillan Publishing Corporation

First published 1991
Aberdeen University Press

© Joyce and Maurice Lindsay 1991

British Library Cataloguing in Publication Data

A catalogue record for this book
is available from the British Library.

ISBN 0 08 041209 2

Typeset by Bookman Limited
Printed by Athenaeum Press Limited

Contents

Preface

A few years ago, when my wife and I produced *The Scottish Dog*, an anthology of the national canine literature, we were astonished to learn from one reviewer that there were 'bits missing'. That, of course, is a fundamental attribute of any anthology, which must inevitably be a personal selection, culled from an almost limitless field of choice. As it happens, very little of literary interest or value written about The Scottish Dog down the ages was, in fact, excluded. *A Pleasure of Gardens*, however, deals with a much wider area of interest and takes in writing about various aspects of gardens and gardening from Scotland, England, Ireland, America, and, indeed, the Ancient World. So vast is the range of choice of available material that many aspects of our subject could not be included. We do not, for example, deal with the world's great gardens, which can only be presented meaningfully in a larger format and with lavish colour illustration. Nor do we deal in detail with narrower specialist matters such as: the lives of the great gardeners (though the thoughts of some of them are included in our pages); the findings of botanists, or the linguistic technicalities of the naming of plants. Instead, what we have tried to do is to hold up a broad mirror of literary delight for ordinary people who enjoy gardens and gardening.

We have divided *A Pleasure of Gardens* into sections, with a brief Proem and Coda by way, so to say, of opening and shutting the gate at the beginning and end of the book.

First, we consider the garden as a 'lovesome thing', to use the famous phrase of the Manx poet, TE Brown. Then follows a section 'Sharing the Garden', in which many of the creatures, welcome or unwelcome, to be found in the garden, are introduced.

Our third section is headed by the old Anglo-Saxon term 'Tussie-Mussie', meaning 'a bunch or posy of flowers', which the *Oxford English Dictionary* describes as obsolete but which that fine English gardener Vita Sackville-West insisted should not be allowed to remain so. We thus play our part in helping to keep the term alive.

Gardens provide a setting for people, especially lovers, many of whom are to be found colourfully here. In some respects the most important figure of all is 'The Gardener'. We therefore give him (or her) a complete section, while another is devoted to the practicalities of the gardener's craft.

Months and seasons rule the gardener's life, with or without the help of the various traditional saws or sayings about them that have come down to us. Each has its own section. To many who enjoy gardens, not the least delight is the concert of 'Birdsong' which they inspire and contain: the birds have a final section to themselves.

All my life I have enjoyed gardens. My enjoyment, however, has been entirely of the passive kind, allowing the effect of colours and scents and particular compositions of flowers to flow over me, like silent music, in a pleasurable wash. Not for me the labours of digging, planting, weeding and trimming; the endless struggle against predators, or the diseases of nature; the memorising of the myriad Latinised names of plants, nor the anxious glance towards a frosting or gathering sky.

My wife, on the other hand, though too modest to lay claim to professional expertise, is the more robustly complete garden-lover. Not only has she made the energetic most of the gardens of varying shapes and sizes that have surrounded our almost half-a-century of homes in Scotland and Cumbria, wherever circumstance has taken us, but she still digs and plants, weeds and usually knows the *what* and the *why* of things that merely delight or astonish me.

This anthology was originally her idea. True to family tradition, in furnishing the contents of the pages she has done most of the digging and weeding, while I have suggested a bloom here, or a bird-note there, and enjoyed savouring the whole. With such a duality of editorial approach, we hope that *A Pleasure of Gardens* will bring delight to gardeners and garden-lovers of every degree of practical involvement—or even none at all.

There are helpers to be thanked. Our old friend Morven Cameron drew the designs in each section. Fran Walker, our neighbour on Milton Hill, not only made contributory suggestions, but also put her professional librarian's knowledge most generously at our disposal. The staff at the Mitchell Library, Glasgow, were, as they always are, unstintingly helpful, in particular, Mr John Eaglesham. Mr Stanley M Simpson and Miss M E Townley of the National Library of Scotland gave us invaluable assistance by locating and making available for our inspection old or rare gardening books long out of print. Mrs Sadie Douglas, the Administrative Director of the Scottish Civic Trust, facilitated the preparation of the final text, in the assembling of which my secretary, Mrs Wilma Bryce, typed patient sense out of the sprawling tendrils of my handwriting.

Maurice Lindsay

Acknowledgements

The editors and publisher are grateful to authors, publishers and other copyright holders whose permission to use copyright material is acknowledged. Every effort has been made to trace all copyright holders (given in brackets), but in a few instances this has proved impossible. Where such work has been included in this anthology, it is with our apologies, and in the belief that its fresh exposure to additional readers will be welcome.

Thanks are due to James Aitchison, 'The Last Clean Bough' and 'In the North' (the poet); Alan Bold, 'Monet's Garden at Giverny' (the poet); Derek Bowman, 'Couch-Grass' (Mrs Marianne Bowman); George Mackay Brown, 'A Child's Calendar' (the poet); George Bruce, 'Snowdrops in March', and 'Robins' (the poet); Walter De la Mare, 'The Bee's Song' (The Society of Authors); Emily Dickinson, 'Bees', 'A Bird Came Down the Walk', and 'Envoi' (Trustees of Amherst College, from *The Poems of Emily Dickinson*, ed Thomas H Johnson, The Belknap Press of Harvard University); Valerie Gillies, 'To a Butterfly in an Overgrown Garden' (the poet and Canongate Press); Oliver St John Gogarty, 'The Apple Tree' (Mr Oliver D Gogarty); Norman Kreitman, 'Designing a Japanese Garden' (the poet); C Day Lewis, 'The Crysanthemum Show' and 'Now the full-throated Daffodils' (estate of C Day Lewis and Jonathan Cape); Norman MacCaig, 'Earwig', 'Toad', 'Caterpillar', 'How to Cover the Ground' and 'Starling on a Green Lawn' (the poet); Hugh MacDiarmid, 'First Love' (Mr Michael Grieve); Edwin Morgan, extract from 'For Bonfires' (the poet and Carcanet Press); Howard Nemerov, 'The Beautiful Lawn Sprinkler', 'A Cabinet of Seeds Displayed' and 'Burning the Leaves' (the poet); Beverley Nichols, 'Cats', 'Peace in the Greenhouse', 'Women Gardeners'; Theodore Roethke, 'Weed Puller' and 'The Siskins' (Faber and Faber); Vita Sackville-West, extract from *The Garden* (Curtis Brown); James Simmons, 'Old Gardener' (the poet); Iain Crichton Smith, 'The Birds' and 'Two Birds' (Carcanet Press); William Soutar, 'For a Sundial', 'Waggletail' and 'Yellow Yorlins' (National Library of Scotland); Wallace Stevens, 'A Room on a Garden' (Faber and Faber); Allen Tate, 'To A Prodigal Old Maid' (Farrar, Straus and Giroux, Inc.); Andrew Waterman, 'Gardens' (the poet); Henry Williamson, from *Goodbye West Country* (A M Heath & Co, London); Andrew Young, 'Through Field

Glasses' (the Andrew Young Estate); Douglas Young, 'Last Lauch' (Mrs Hella Young).

Proem

The Greatest Service

The greatest service which can be rendered any country is to add a useful plant to its culture.

THOMAS JEFFERSON

Well Said

'Tis well said,' said Candide, 'and now we must cultivate our garden.'

VOLTAIRE

A Sprig of Grass

There is not a sprig of grass that shoots uninteresting to me.

THOMAS JEFFERSON

The First Garden

God the first garden made, and the first city Cain.

ABRAHAM COWLEY

A Delight to the Eye

A garden is a delight to the eye, and a solace to the soul; it soothes angry passions, and produces that pleasure which is a foretaste of paradise.

MARIE FRANÇOIS SADI CARNOT ('Sadi')

A LOVESOME THING

A Heaven on Earth

A Heaven on Earth: for blissful Paradise
Of God the garden was, by him in the east
Of Eden planted...
Out of the fertile ground he caus'd to grow
All trees of noblest kind for sight, smell, taste:
And all amid there stood the tree of life,
High eminent, blooming ambrosial fruit
Of vegetable gold: and next to life
Our death, the tree of knowledge, grew fast by...
Knowledge of good bought dear by knowing ill.

JOHN MILTON

The First Garden

God Almighty first planted a Garden; and indeed it is the purest of humane pleasures. It is the greatest refreshment to the Spirits of Man, without which Buildings and Palaces are but gross Handyworks. And a Man shall ever see, that when Ages grow to Civility and Elegancy, Men come to build stately, sooner than to garden finely: as if Gardening were the Greater Perfection. I do hold it in the Royal Ordering of Gardens, there ought to be Gardens for all the Months in the Year, in which, severally, things of Beauty may be then in season.

For December and January, and the latter part of November, you must take such things as are green all Winter: Holly, Ivy, Bays, Juniper, Cypress-Trees, Yews, Pine-Apple Trees, Fir-Trees, Rosemary, Lavender, Periwinckle, the White, the Purple, and the Blue, Germander, Flags, Orange-Trees, Limon-Trees, and Myrtles, if they be stirred, and Sweet Marjoram warm set.

There followeth, for the latter part of January and February, the Mezerion Tree, which then blossoms, Crocus Vernus, both the Yellow and the Grey, Prim-Roses, Anemones, the Early Tulippa, Hiacynthus Orientalis, Chamaïris, Frettellaria.

For March, there come Violets, specially the Single Blue, which are the Earliest, the yellow Daffadil, the Daisy, the Almond-Tree in blossom, the Peach-Tree in blossom, the Cornelian-Tree in blossom, Sweet Briar.

In April follow the double White Violet, the Wall-Flower, the Stock-Gilly-Flower, the Cowslip, Flower-de-Lices, and Lilies of all natures, Rosemary-Flowers, the Tulippa, the Double Piony, the pale Daffadill, the French Honey-Suckle, the Cherry-Tree in blossom, the Dammasin and Plum-Trees in blossom, the White Thorn in leaf, the Lelack Tree.

In May and June, come Pinks of all Sorts, specially the Blush-Pink, Roses of all kinds (except the Musk, which comes later), Honey-Suckles, Strawberries, Bugloss, Columbine, the French Marygold, Flos Africanus, Cherry-Tree in fruit, Ribes, Figs in fruit, Rasps, Vine-Flowers, Lavender in Flowers, the Sweet Satyrion with the White Flower, Herba Muscaria, Lillium Convallium, the Apple-Tree in blossom.

In July come Gilly-Flowers of all Varieties, Musk-Roses, and the Lime-Tree in blossom, Early Pears and Plumbs in fruit, Ginnitings, Quodlings.

In August, come Plumbs of all sorts in Fruit, Pears, Apricocks, Barberries, Filberds, Musk-Melons, Monkshoods of all Colours.

In September come Grapes, Apples, Poppies of all Colours, Peaches, Melo-Cotones, Nectarines, Cornellians, Wardens, Quinces.

In October and the beginning of November come Servises, Medlars, Bullaces; Roses Cut or Removed to come late, Holly-oaks, and such like.

These particulars are for the climate of London: But my meaning is perceived, that you may have *Ver Perpetuum*, as the place affords.

FRANCIS BACON

The First Gift

When God did man to his own likeness make,
As much as clay, though of the purest kind,
By the great Potter's art refin'd,
Could the Divine impression take,
He thought it fit to place him, where
A kind of heaven too did appear,
As far as earth could such a likeness bear:
That man no happiness might want,

Which earth to her first master could afford;
He did a garden for him plant
By the quick hand of his omnipotent word.
As the chief help and joy of human life,
He gave him the first gift; first ev'n before a wife.

ABRAHAM COWLEY

Gardening

I have often thought that if heaven had given me choice of my position and calling, it should have been on a rich spot of earth, well watered, and near a good market for the productions of the garden. No occupation is so delightful to me as the culture of the earth, and no culture comparable to that of the garden. Such a variety of subjects, some one always coming to perfection, the failure of one thing repaired by the success of another, and instead of one harvest a continued one through the year. Under a total want of demand except for our family table, I am still devoted to the garden. But though an old man, I am but a young gardener.

THOMAS JEFFERSON

Beauties in Flowers, Curiosities in Plants

Most certain it is, amongst all these transitory entertainments of our lives, there is none more suitable to the mind of man than this; for I dare boldly assert, that if there be anyone that is become so much a herbarist as to be delighted with the pleasant aspects of nature, so as to have walked a few turns in her solitary places, traced her alleys, viewed her several embroidered beds, recreated and feasted himself with her fragrances, the harmless delights of her fields and gardens; he it is that hath embraced one of the greatest of our terrestrial felicities. Hence it is, that emperors, princes, heroes, and persons of the most generous qualifications have trod on their sceptres, slighted their thrones, cast away their purples, and laid aside all other exuberances of state, to court their Mother Earth in her own dressings: such beauties there are to be discovered in flowers, such curiosities of features to be found in plants.

WILLIAM COLES

The Earth Apparalled

For if delight may provoke men's labour, what greater delight is there than to behold the earth apparalled with plants, as with a robe of embroidered work, set with Orient pearls and garnished with great diversity of rare and costly jewels? If this variety and perfection of colours may affect the eye, it is such in herbs and flowers that no Appelles, no Zeuxis, ever could by any art express the like: if odours or if taste may work satisfaction they are both so sovereign in plants and so comfortable that no confection of the apothecaries can equal their excellent virtue. But these delights are in the outward senses; the principal delight is in the mind, singularly enriched with the knowledge of these visible things, setting forth to us the invisible wisdom and admirable workmanship of Almighty God.

JOHN GERARDE

Garden Delights

The Turks who passed their Days in Gardens here, will have Gardens also hereafter; and delighting in Flowers on Earth, must have Lilies and Roses in Heaven. In Garden Delights it is not easy to hold a Mediocrity; that insinuating Pleasure is seldom without some Extremity. The Ancients venially delighted in flourishing Gardens. Many were Florists that knew not the true use of a Flower. And in Pliny's Days none had directly treated of that Subject. Some commendably affected Plantations of venomous Vegetables; some confined their delights unto single Plants; and Cato seemed to dote upon Cabbage. While the ingenius Delight of Tulipists, stands saluted with hard language, even by their own Professors.

SIR THOMAS BROWNE

Free From Care

What boots it to wear out the soul with anxious thoughts? I want not wealth; I want not power; heaven is beyond my hopes. Then let me stroll through the bright hours as they pass in my garden among my flowers...Thus will I work out my allotted space, content with appointments of Fate, my spirit free from care.

LAO CH'IEN

Each Its Own Character

Every garden has its own special and separate character, which arises partly from the tastes of the owner or his gardener, but still more from the situation, aspect, and soil of the garden. It is this that saves our gardens from monotony; if the conditions of every garden were the same, it is to be feared that the love of following the fashion of the day would make our gardens painfully alike. But this is prevented by the happy law that before success can be reached the nature of the garden must be studied, and the study soon leads to the conviction that we cannot take our neighbour's garden as the exact model of our own, but must be content to learn a little from one and a little from another, and then to adapt the lessons to our own garden in the way that our experience (often very dearly bought) tells us is the best. And because of this special character in each separate garden it follows that each garden has something to teach, which cannot be taught so well elsewhere; and the happy result is that no one with a love for gardening who visits other gardens with his eyes open can ever go into a garden (especially if the owner of that garden is a true lover of flowers) without learning something. And it is this that makes the records of good gardens such pleasant reading; we cannot all go to Lancashire, Scotland, or the Thames valley, but we can be thankful for the records of the gardens in those places.

CANON HENRY ELLACOMBE

Beauty and Delight

There is no spot of ground, however arid, or ugly, that cannot be tamed into such a state as may give an impression of beauty and delight. It cannot always be done easily; many things worth doing are not done easily, but there is no place under natural conditions that cannot be graced with an adornment of suitable vegetation.

GERTRUDE JEKYLL

Plants Speaking

What a pleasure it is for a man (whom the ignorant think to be alone) to have plants speaking Greek and Latin to him and putting him in mind of stories which otherwise he would never think of.

WILLIAM COLES

The Fascination of Plant Names

The fascination of plant names is founded on two instincts—love of nature and curiosity about language.

REV JOHN EARLE

Old Names

I favour old names and I am pleased my gardener, James Spalding, should use them. Though in other ways he is a silent man he talks to children, animals and flowers. Yesternoon he told me five names for the Pansy to which I did add a sixth, Pensé for a thought, yet he would have none of it. Herb Trinity he calls them, and Three Faces under a Hood, and Love in Idleness, Stepmother, and Hearts Ease. A peasant will make his Poetry out of the Earth how ever hard times may be.

DION CLAYTON CALTHORP

Innocent Delights

You must know, Sir, that I look upon the pleasure which we take in a Garden, as one of the most innocent delights in human life. A Garden was the habitation of our first parents before the fall. It is naturally apt to fill the mind with calmness and tranquillity, and to lay all its turbulent passions at rest. It gives us a great insight into the contrivance and wisdom of providence, and suggests innumerable subjects for meditation. I cannot but think the very complacency and satisfaction which a man takes in these works of Nature to be a laudable if not a virtuous habit of mind.

JOSEPH ADDISON

Forms and Arrangements

Nature affords us but few materials to work with. Plants, ground and water, are her only productions; and though both the forms and arrangement of these may be varied to an incredible degree, yet have they but few striking varieties, the rest being of the nature of changes rung upon bells ... Art must therefore supply the scantiness of nature; and not only be employed to produce variety, but also novelty and effect: for the simple arrangements of nature are ... too familiar to excite any strong sensation in the mind of the beholder, or to produce any uncommon degree of pleasure.

SIR WILLIAM CHAMBERS

A Key to Right Thinking

It will be a key to right thinking about gardens if you will consider in what places a garden is most desired. In a very beautiful country, especially if it be mountainous, we can do without it well enough; whereas in a flat and dull country we crave after it, and there it is often the very making of the homestead. While in great towns, gardens, both private and public, are positive necessities if the citizens are to live reasonable and healthy lives in body and mind.

WILLIAM MORRIS

Garden Seclusion

The garden, in every language, speaks of seclusion. To flower and plant and tree, it is a cloistered refuge from the battle of life, a paradise where free from the pinch of poverty and the malice of their enemies, they may turn their thoughts and their strength from war to beauty; and this perfect freedom of the garden finds a voice in the joyous murmur of the fountain, for water too is outside the struggle for existence, and goes on its way rejoicing from one ocean of darkness to another. So, to man, the garden should be something without and beyond nature; a page from an old romance, a scene in fairyland, a gateway through which imaginations lifted above the sombre reality of life may pass into the world of dreams. One should be able to escape to it from labour or business, from office or Senate-house or study, as to a haven of rest and refreshment, where time does not dole out his seconds to you like a miser telling his guineas, nor snatch again the golden moments you cannot hold; no sound of the outer world should break the enchantment; no turret-clock should toll the passing hour; nor, could one silence it, should there vibrate through the garden the menacing voice of the church bell, with its muttered curse on nature and on man, lest it beat down the petals of the pagan roses.

SIR GEORGE SITWELL

Two Pleasures

The Green hath two pleasures; the one because nothing is more pleasant to the Eye than Green Grass kept finely shorn; the other because it will give you a fair Alley in the midst, by which you may go in front upon a Stately Hedge, which is to enclose the Garden. But because the Alley will be long, and in great Heat of the Year or Day, you ought not to buy the shade in the Garden, by going in the Sun through the Green; therefore you are, of either Side the Green, to plant a Covert Alley upon Carpenter's Work, about twelve foot in Height, by which you may go in shade into the Garden. As for the making of Knots or Figures, with Divers Coloured Earths, that they may lie under the Windows of the House, on that Side which the Garden stands, they be but Toys, you may see as good sights many times in Tarts.

FRANCIS BACON

Requisites for Perfection

The perfection of landscape gardening consists in the four following requisites: *First*, it must display the natural beauties, and hide the natural defects of every situation. *Secondly*, it should give the appearance of extent and freedom, by carefully disguising or hiding the boundary. *Thirdly*, it must studiously conceal every interference of art, however expressed, by which the natural scenery is imposed; making the whole appear the production of nature only; and *fourthly*, all objects of mere convenience or comfort, if incapable of being made ornamental, or of becoming proper parts of the general scenery, must be removed or concealed.

·HUMPHREY REPTON

In Just Order

To deck the shapely knoll
That, softly swell'd and gaily dress'd, appears
A flow'ry island from the dark green lawn
Emerging, must be deem'd a labour due
To no mean hand, and asks the touch of taste.
Here also grateful mixture of well match'd
And sorted hues (each giving each relief,
And by contrasted beauty shining more)
Is needful. Strength may wield the pond'rous spade,
May turn the clod, and wheel the compost home,
But elegance, chief grace the garden shows
And most attractive, is the fair result
Of thought, the creature of a polish'd mind.
Without it, all is Gothic as the scene
To which th' insipid citizen resorts
Near yonder heath; where industry misspent,
But proud of his uncouth, ill-chosen task,
Has made a heaven on earth; with suns and moons
Of close-ramm'd stones has charged th' encumber'd soil
And fairly laid the zodiac in the dust.

He, therefore, who would see his flow'rs disposed
Sightly and in just order, ere he gives
The beds the trusted treasure of their seeds,
Forecasts the future whole; that when the scene
Shall break into its preconceived display,
Each for itself, and all as with one voice
Conspiring, may attest his bright design.
Nor even then, dismissing as perform'd
His pleasant work, may he suppose it done.
Few self-supported flow'rs endure the wind
Uninjured, but expect th' upholding aid
Of the smooth-shaven prop, and neatly tied
Are wedded thus, like beauty to old age,
For int'rest sake, the living to the dead.
Some clothe the soil that feeds them, far diffused
And lowly creeping, modest and yet fair;
Like virtue, thriving most where little seen.
Some, more aspiring, catch the neighbour shrub
With clasping tendrils, and invest his branch,
Else unadorn'd, with many a gay festoon
And fragrant chaplet, recompensing well
The strength they borrow with the grace they lend.
All hate the rank society of weeds,
Noisome, and ever greedy to exhaust
Th' impov'rish'd earth; and overbearing race,
That, like the multitude made faction-mad,
Disturb good order, and degrade true worth.

WILLIAM COWPER

English Privacy

The English detest being seen and will gladly forego any prospect beyond their own limited boundaries... One cannot hope to
have the pleasure of seeing passers-by on the highway, travellers, labourers working in the fields, or the glimpse of a village and the adjacent landscape. Green lawns and flower-beds
with superb trees which obscure all view, that is what the English like.

DUCHESSE DE DINO

The Garden

How vainly men themselves amaze
To win the palm, the oak, or bays,
And their uncessant labours see
Crown'd from some single herb or tree,
Whose short and narrow-vergéd shade
Does prudently their toils upbraid;
While all the flowers and trees do close
To weave the garlands of repose.

Fair Quiet, have I found thee here,
And Innocence thy sister dear!
Mistaken long, I sought you then
In busy companies of men:
Your sacred plants, if here below,
Only among the plants will grow:
Society is all but rude
To this delicious solitude.

No white or red was ever seen
So amorous as this lovely green.
Fond lovers, cruel as their flame,
Cut in these trees their mistress' name:
Little, alas, they know or heed
How far these beauties hers exceed!
Fair trees! wheres'e'er your barks I wound,
No name shall but your own be found.

When we have run our passions' heat
Love hither makes his best retreat:
The gods, who mortal beauty chase,
Still in a tree did end their race:
Apollo hunted Daphne so,
Only that she might laurel grow:
And Pan did after Syrinx speed
Not as a nymph, but for a reed.

What wondrous life in this I lead!
Ripe apples drop about my head;
The luscious clusters of the vine
Upon my mouth do crush their wine;

The nectarine and curious peach
Into my hands themselves do reach;
Stumbling on melons, as I pass,
Ensnared with flowers, I fall on grass.

Meanwhile the mind, from pleasure less,
Withdraw into its happiness;
The mind, that ocean where each kind
Does straight its own resemblance find;
Yet it creates, transcending these,
Far other worlds, and other seas;
Annihilating all that's made
To a green thought in a green shade.

Here at the fountain's sliding foot
Or at some fruit-tree's mossy root,
Casting the body's vest aside,
My soul into the boughs does glide;
There, like a bird, it sits and sings,
Then whets and claps its silver wings,
And, till prepared for longer flight,
Waves in its plumes the various light.

Such was that happy Garden-state
While man there walk'd without a mate:
After a place so pure and sweet,
What other help could yet be meet!
But 'twas beyond a mortal's share
To wander solitary there:
Two paradises 'twere in one,
To live in Paradise alone.

How well the skilful gardener drew
Of flowers and herbs this dial new!
Where, from above, the milder sun
Does through a fragrant Zodiac run:
And, as it works, th' industrious bee
Computes its time as well as we.
How could such sweet and wholesome hours
Be reckon'd, but with herbs and flowers!

ANDREW MARVELL

The Cottage Garden

English cottage gardens are never bare and seldom ugly. Those who look at sea or sky or wood see beauty that no art can show; but among the things made by man nothing is prettier than an English cottage garden, and they often teach lessons that 'great' gardeners should learn, and are pretty from snowdrop time till the Fuchsia bushes bloom nearly into winter. We do not see the same thing in other lands...

What is the secret of the cottage garden's charm? Cottage gardeners are good to their plots, and in the course of years they make them fertile, and the shelter of the little house and hedge favours the flowers. But there is something more and it is the absence of any pretentious 'plan', which lets the flowers tell their story to the heart.

Of the many things that should be thought of in the making of a garden to live in, this of fragance is one of the first... Apart from the groups of plants in which all, or nearly all, are fragrant, as in Roses, the annual and biennial flowers of our gardens are rich in fragrance—Stocks, Mignonette, Sweet Peas, Sweet Sultan, Wallflowers, double Rockets, Sweet Scabious, and many others. These, among the most easily raised of plants, may be enjoyed by the poorest cottage gardeners.

WILLIAM ROBINSON

The Garden of Pleasure

The most pleasant and delectable thing for recreation belonging unto our farmes is our flower gardens... It is a commendable and seemely thing to behold out at a window many acres of ground well tilled and husbanded... But yet it is much more to behold faire and comely proportions, handsome and pleasant arboures and as it were closets, delightfull borders of lavender, rosemarie, boxe, and other such like: to heare the ravising musicke of an infinite number of prettie small birdes, which continually day and night doe chatter and chant their proper and naturall branch songs upon the hedges and trees of the garden: and to smell so sweet a nosegaie so neere at hand: seeing that this so fragant a smell cannot but refresh the Lord of the farme exceedingly, when going out of his bed-chamber in the morning after the sunne-rise, and whiles as yet the cleere and pearlelike dew doth pearch unto the grasse. He giveth himself to heare the melodious musicke of the Bees: which busying themselves in gathering of the same, do also fill the aire with a most acceptable, sweet and pleasant harmonie: besides the borders and continued rows of soveraigne, thyme, balme, rosemarie, marierome, cypers, soothernwood, and other fragrant herbes, the sight and view whereof cannot but give great contentment unto the beholder.

CHARLES ESTIENNE

The Allotment Garden

In the winter, they have rather a desolate aspect, with their naked trees and hedges and all their little summer-houses exposed, damp-looking and forlorn; but in spring and summer they look exceedingly well, —in spring, all starred with blossoms, all thick with leaves; and their summer-houses peeping pleasantly from among them. The advantage of these gardens to the working-class of a manufacturing town (Nottingham) is beyond calculation...

Early in spring, they get into their gardens, tidy, clear and dig. Trees are pruned, beds are dug, walks cleaned, and all the refuse and decayed vegetables piled up in heaps...

Every garden has its summer-house; and these are of all scales and grades, from the erection of a few tub-staves, with an attempt to train a pumpkin or a wild-hop over it, to substantial brick houses with glass windows, good cellars for a deposit of choice wines, a kitchen and all necessary apparatus, and a good pump to supply them with water. Many are very picturesque rustic huts, built with great taste, and hidden by tall hedges in a perfect little paradise of lawn and shrubbery.

WILLIAM HOWITT

The Roof Garden

A nervous hose is dribbling on the tar
This morning on this rooftop where I'm watching you
Move among your sparse, pinchpenny flowers,
Poor metronomes of color one month long
That pull the sun's rays in as best they can
And suck life up from one mere inch of dirt.
There's water in the sky but it won't come down.

Once we counted the skyline's water towers,
Barrels made of shingle, fat and high,
An African village suspended above
The needle hardness of New York that needs
More light than God provides to make it soft,
That needs the water in the water towers
To snake through pipe past all the elevators
To open up in bowls and baths and showers.

Soon our silence will dissolve in talk,
In talk that needs some water and some sun,
Or it will go the same way as before:
Dry repetitions of the ill we bear
Each other, the baited poles of light
Angling through the way the sun today
Fishes among the clouds.

Now you are through
Watering geraniums, and now you go
To the roof edge to survey the real estate
Of architectured air—tense forms wrought up,
Torn down, replaced, to be torn down again...
So much like us. Your head against the sky
Is topped by a tower clock, blocks away,
Whose two black hands are closing on the hour,
And I look down into the street below,
Rinsed fresh this morning by a water truck,
Down which a girl, perky in high heels,
Clops by, serenely unaware of us,
Of the cables, gas lines, telephone wires,
And water mains, writhing underfoot.

HOWARD MOSS

In a Chinese Garden

I took money and bought flowering trees
And planted them out on the bank to the east of the Keep.
I simply bought whatever had most blooms,
Not caring whether peach, apricot, or plum.
A hundred fruits, all mixed up together;
A thousand branches, flowering in due rotation.
Each has its season coming early or late;
But to all alike the fertile soil is kind.
The red flowers hang like a heavy mist;
The white flowers gleam like a fall of snow.
The wandering bees cannot bear to leave them;
The sweet birds also come there to roost.
In front there flows an ever-running stream:
Beneath there is built a little flat terrace.
Sometimes I sweep the flagstones of the terrace;
Sometimes, in the wind, I raise my cup and drink.
The flower-branches screen my head from the sun;
The flower-buds fall down into my lap.
Alone drinking, alone singing my songs,
I do not notice that the moon is level with the steps.
The people of Pa do not care for flowers;
All the spring no one has come to look.
But their Governor-General, alone with his cup of wine,
Sits till evening, and will not move from the place!

PO-CHÜ-I

Designing A Japanese Garden

First you must ask disturbing questions;
do you, for example, insist on walking about
    or have you acquired
enough understanding to stay in one place?

Then consider purpose. Presumably the garden
will chiefly be used for poetry competitions,
    or will you drink tea,
or instead, think of the verities of the Masters?

Decide next on what is within, what is out,
how light shall enter the eye of the house
    when shadows lean outwards,
where the floor will end and the world begin.

And clarify your thoughts concerning the open air;
need you borrow space from the hazy mountains
    or is the nearer sky enough?
Would a wall help to block and organise your seeing?

Then you may set your garden, but choose to show
chiefly those truths which are assymetrical;
    pain need not appear
but have water for balm, rushes for consolation.

Finally, place the massive stone,
and let that be your gravity.

                              NORMAN KREITMAN

Gardens

'This is your garden. Dig it.'
Eight hummocky feet by three in a rancid corner.
Bored, I poked about, chopped at worms, bought seeds

at Woolworth's in vividly illustrated packets.
Such as came up looked shoddier, or were just weeds.
And besides, I preferred running off down the forest.

Since then I've had no gardens, 'And no regrets,'
I usually say, 'they enslave you.'
All those bank-clerks pruning their privet each Sunday!

Not but what peering in on some shimmering lawn
with water-sprinklers rotating for ever, splodged
with immaculate flowerbeds, there's not envy—

though the silver-haired bloke at the roller framed against
open french windows is not my style,
nor such casual-seeming perfectedness, not to mention

rustic bird-baths, phoney tudor lanterns.
Still, as I move on, does the wrought-iron of his gate
bar his world or mine? I wonder.

And I quite like to haunt public gardens;
or those of stately homes, with statuary,
ornamental cascades and grottoes, hedges cut

into classically soluble mazes,
or some landscaped romantic vista along a lake,
trees shovelled up into the clouds.

And back looking out of whatever rooms I've got
at some rubbly yard with bins, or untended jungle
where you hear the tumbledown walls' stones grinding in frost,

I hanker after illusive gardens,
from Adam and Eve to *Alice*; and that one
in the story everyone's read, through a magical gate

in a wall in a drab city street.
Some fertile green congruence: I can almost feel
its moss, catch scents in the breeze, hear the sound of water.

'Concrete the bloody things over and leave yourself free.'
Yet now, if I found myself settling for one,
I'd set about digging.

ANDREW WATERMAN

The Faults of Gardening

Now the faults of gardening,...all centre in this one thing—the
constant subjection of the imaginative, or higher, to the sensuous,
or lower, element of flower beauty. We will trace this, first, in the
general arrangement of gardens and of flowers in relation to each
other, and afterwards in the case of their individual culture. To begin,

then, we find flower-beds habitually considered too much as mere masses of colour, instead of an assemblage of living beings. The only thought is to delight the eye by the utmost possible splendour. When we walk in our public gardens everything seems tending to distract the attention from the separate plants, and to make us look at them only with regard to their united effect. And this univeral brilliancy, this striking effect of the masses, is the acknowledged chief aim of the cultivator...

Has any of our readers, gifted with real love for flowers, ever walked through one of those older gardens, and observed the wide difference in its effect? I am not here speaking necessarily of the grounds of a mansion, but merely of such a garden as might often be found, some twenty years ago, attached to any good-sized house in a country town or village. Or even a little cottage-plot of the kind so beautifully described by Clare will to some extent illustrate my meaning:

> And where the marjoram once, and sage and rue,
> And balm and mint, with curled-leaf parsley grew,
> And double marigolds, and silver thyme,
> And pumpkins 'neath the window used to climb;
> And where I often, when a child, for hours
> Tried through the pales to get the tempting flowers;
> As lady's laces everlasting peas,
> True love lies bleeding, with the hearts at ease;
> And golden rods, and tansy running high,
> That o'er the pale top smiled on passer-by;
> Flowers in my time which every one would praise,
> Though thrown like weeds from gardens now-a-days.

There might be but little attempt at colour-grouping, or at the production of effect by masses in a narrow sense. But was there any want of beauty there? And did you not feel, in looking at those flowers, how each made you love it as a friend—the Pinks and Sweet Williams, the Everlasting Peas, Valerian, Day Lily, Jacob's Ladder, and a host of others? And did you not notice how ever and again you fell upon some quaint, strange plant which has been expelled from the modern border, which seemed to touch your inmost soul, and to fill the mind, especially if in childhood, with a sense of wonder and mysterious awe?

FORBES WATSON

Consult the Genius of the Place

Something there is, more needful than Expence,
And something previous ev'n to Taste—'tis Sense:
Good Sense, which only is the gift of Heav'n,
And tho' no Science, fairly worth the seven:
A light, which in yourself you must perceive:
Jones and Le Nôtre have it not to give.
    To build, to plant, whatever you intend,
To rear the Column, or the Arch to bend,
To swell the Terras, or to sink the Grot;
In all, let Nature never be forgot.
But treat the Goddess like a modest fair,
Nor over-dress, nor leave her wholly bare,
Let not each beauty ev'ry where be spy'd,
Where half the skill is decently to hide.
He gains all points, who pleasingly confounds,
Surprizes, varies, and conceals the Bounds.
    Consult the Genius of the Place in all;
That tells the Waters or to rise, or fall,
Or helps th'ambitious Hill the heav'ns to scale,
Or scoops in circling theatres the Vale;
Calls in the Country, catches op'ning glades,
Joins willing woods, and varies shades from shades;
Now breaks, or now directs, th'intending lines,
Paints as you plant, and as you work, designs.

ALEXANDER POPE

Improving Pope's Garden

Sir William Stanhope was persuaded...to *improve* Pope's garden...
The poet had valued himself on the disposition of it, and with reason.
Though containing but five acres, enclosed by three lanes, he had
managed it with such art and deception, that it seemed a wood and
its boundaries were nowhere discoverable...Refined taste went to
work: the vocal groves were thinned, modish shrubs replaced them
and light and three lanes broke in; and if the Muses wanted to tie up
their garters, there is not a nook to do it without being seen.

HORACE WALPOLE

Miraculous!

Mr Milestone.–This, you perceive, is the natural state of one part of the grounds. Here is a wood, never yet touched by the finger of taste; thick, intricate, gloomy. Here is a little stream, dashing from stone to stone, and overshadowed with these untrimmed boughs.

Miss Tenorina.–The sweet romantic spot! How beautifully the birds must sing there on a summer evening!

Miss Graziosa.–Dear sister! How can you endure the horrid thicket?

Mr Milestone.–You are right, Miss Graziosa; your taste is correct, perfectly *en règle*. Now, here is the same place corrected –trimmed–polished–decorated–adorned. Here sweeps a plantation, in that beautiful regular curve; there winds a gravel walk; here are parts of the old wood, left in these majestic circular clumps, disposed at equal distances with wonderful symmetry; there are some singular shrubs scattered in elegant profusion; here a Portugal laurel, there a juniper; here a laurustinus, there a spruce fir; here a larch, there a lilac; here a rhododendron, there an arbutus. The stream, you see, is become a canal: the banks are perfectly smooth and green, sloping to the water's edge: and there is Lord Littlebrain, rowing in an elegant boat.

Squire Headlong.–Magical, faith!

Mr Milestone.–Here is another part of the ground in its natural state. Here is a large rock, with the mountain-ash rooted in its fissures, over-grown, as you see, with ivy and moss, and from this part of it bursts a little fountain, that runs bubbling down its rugged sides.

Miss Tenorina.–O how beautiful! How I should love the melody of that miniature cascade!

Mr Milestone.–Beautiful, Miss Tenorina! Hideous. Base, common, and popular. Such a thing as you may see anywhere, in wild and mountainous districts. Now, observe the metamorphosis. Here is the same rock, cut into the shape of a giant. In one hand he holds a horn, through which the little fountain is thrown to a prodigious elevation. In the other is a ponderous stone, so exactly balanced as to be apparently ready to fall on the head of any person who may happen to be beneath, and there is Lord Littlebrain walking under it.

Squire Headlong.–Miraculous, by Mahomet!

THOMAS LOVE PEACOCK

How Beautiful, How Welcome

She went, however, and they sauntered about together many an half hour in Mrs Grant's shrubbery, the weather being unusually mild for the time of year, and venturing sometimes even to sit down on one of the benches now comparatively unsheltered, remaining there perhaps till, in the midst of some tender ejaculation of Fanny's on the sweets of so protracted an autumn, they were forced by the sudden swell of a cold gust shaking down the last few yellow leaves about them, to jump up and walk for warmth.

'This is pretty, very pretty,' said Fanny, looking around her as they were thus sitting together one day; 'every time I come into this shrubbery I am more struck with its growth and beauty. Three years ago this was nothing but a rough hedgerow along the upper side of the field, never thought of as anything, or capable of becoming anything; and now it is converted into a walk, and it would be difficult to say whether most valuable as a convenience or an ornament; and perhaps in another three years we may be forgetting–almost forgetting what it was before.'...

'It may seem impertinent in me to praise, but I must admire the taste Mrs Grant has shewn in all this. There is such a quiet simplicity in the plan of the walk! Not too much attempted!'

'Yes,' replied Miss Crawford, carelessly, 'It does very well for a place of this sort. One does not think of extent *here*; and between ourselves, till I came to Mansfield, I had not imagined a country parson ever aspired to a shrubbery, or anything of the kind.'

'I am so glad to see the evergreens thrive!' said Fanny, in reply. 'My uncle's gardener always says the soil here is better than his own, and so it appears from the growth of the laurels and evergreens in general. The evergreen! How beautiful, how welcome, how wonderful the evergreen! When one thinks of it, how astonishing a variety of nature! In some countries we know that the tree that sheds its leaf is the variety, but that does not make it less amazing, that the same soil and the same sun should nurture plants differing in the first rule and law of their existence.'

JANE AUSTEN

'Midst Shaven Lawns

Oft when I've seen some lonely mansion stand,
Fresh from the improver's desolating hand,
'Midst shaven lawns, that far around it creep
In one eternal undulating sweep;
And scatter'd clumps, that nod at one another,
Each stiffly waving to its formal brother;
Tired with the extensive scene, so dull and bare,
To Heaven devoutly I've address'd my prayer,
Again the moss-grown terraces to raise,
And spread the labyrinth's perplexing maze;
Replace in even lines the ductile yew,
And plant again the ancient avenue.
Some features then, at least, we should obtain,
To mark this flat, insipid, waving plain;
Some vary'd tints and forms would intervene,
To break this uniform, eternal green.
E'en the trimm'd hedges, that inclosed the field,
Some consolation to the eye might yield;
But even these are studiously removed,
And clumps and bareness only are approved.

RICHARD PAYNE KNIGHT

Garden Mania

The kitchen garden was to be next admired, and he led the way to it across a small portion of the park.

The number of acres contained in this garden was such as Catherine could not listen to without dismay, being more than double the extent of all Mr Allen's as well as her father's, including churchyard and orchard. The walls seemed countless in number, endless in length; a village of hot-houses seemed to arise among them, and a whole parish to be at work within the enclosure. The General was flattered by her look of surprise, which told him almost as plainly, as he soon forced her to tell him in words, that she had never seen any gardens at all equal to them before; and he then modestly owned that, 'without any ambition of that sort himself, without any solicitude about it, he did believe them to be unrivalled in the kingdom. If he had a hobby-horse it was *that*. He loved a garden. Though careless enough in most matters of eating, he loved good fruit; or if he did not, his friends and children did. There were great vexations, however, attending such a garden as his. The utmost care could not always secure the most valuable fruits. The pinery had yielded only one hundred in the last year. Mr Allen, he supposed, must feel these inconveniences as well as himself.'

'No, not at all. Mr Allen did not care about the garden, and never went into it.'

With a triumphant smile of self-satisfaction, the General wished he could do the same, for he never entered his without being vexed in some way or other, by its falling short of his plan.

'How were Mr Allen's succession-houses worked?' describing the nature of his own as they entered them.

'Mr Allen had only one small hot-house, which Mrs Allen had the use of for her plants in winter, and there was a fire in it now and then.'

'He is a happy man!' said the General, with a look of very happy contempt.

Having taken her into every division, and led her under every wall, till she was heartily weary of seeing and wondering, he suffered the girls at last to seize the advantage of an outer door, and then expressing his wish to examine the effect of some recent alterations about the tea-house, proposed it as no unpleasant extension of their walk.

JANE AUSTEN

In My Garden

In my garden three ways meet,
  Thrice the spot is blest;
Hermit thrush comes there to build,
  Carrier doves to nest.

There broad-armed oaks, the copses' maze,
  The cold sea-wind detain;
Here sultry Summer over-stays
  When Autumn chills the plain.

Self-sown my stately garden grows;
  The wind and wind-blown seed,
Cold April rain and colder snows
  My hedges plant and feed.

From mountains far and valleys near
  The harvest sown to-day
Thrive in all weathers without fear,—
  Wild planters, plant away!

In cities high the careful crowds
  Of woe-worn mortals darkling go,
But in these sunny solitudes
  My quiet roses blow.

Methought the sky looked scornful down
  On all was base in man,
And airy tongues did taunt the town,
  'Achieve our peace who can!'

What need I holier dew
  Than Walden's haunted wave,
Distilled from heaven's alembic blue
  Steeped in each forest cave?

If Thought unlock her mysteries,
  If Friendship on me smile,
I walk in marble galleries,
  I talk with Kings the while.

R W EMERSON

Meanwhile My Beans

Meanwhile my beans, the length of whose rows, added together, was seven miles already planted, were impatient to be hoed for the earliest had grown considerably before the latest were in the ground; indeed, they were not easily to be put off. What was the meaning of this so steady and self-respecting, this small Herculean labour, I knew not. I came to love my rows, my beans, though so many more than I wanted. They attached me to the Earth, and so I got strength like Antoeus. But why should I raise them? Only Heaven knows. This was my curious labour all summer—to make this portion of the Earth's surface, which had yielded only cinquefoil, blackberries, johnswort, and the like before, sweet wild fruits and pleasant flowers, produce instead this pulse? What shall I learn of beans or beans of me? I cherish them, I owe them, early and late I have an eye to them, and this is my day's work. It is a fine broad leaf to look on.

HENRY DAVID THOREAU

A Deep Satisfaction

My garden, that skirted the avenue of the Manse, was of precisely the right extent. An hour or two of morning labour was all that it required. But I used to visit and revisit it a dozen times a day, and stand in deep contemplation over my vegetable progeny, with a love that nobody could share or conceive of, who had never taken part in the process of creation.

It was one of the most bewitching sights in the world to observe a hill of beans thrusting through the soil, or a row of early peas just peeping forth sufficiently to trace a line of delicate green. Later in the season the humming-birds were attracted by the blossoms of a peculiar variety of bean; and they were a joy to me, those little spiritual visitants, for deigning to sip airy food out of my nectar-cups. Multitudes of bees used to bury themselves in the yellow blossoms of the summer-squashes.

This, too, was a deep satisfaction; although, when they had laden themselves with sweets, they flew away to some unknown hive, which would give back nothing in requital of what my garden had contributed. But I was glad thus to fling a benefaction upon the passing breeze with the certainty that somebody must profit by it, and that there would be a little more honey in the world to allay the sourness and bitterness which mankind is always complaining of. Yes, indeed; my life was the sweeter for that honey.

NATHANIEL HAWTHORNE

An Open Gate

As he walked one evening, a garden gate, usually closed, stood open; and lo! within, a great red hawthorn, in full flower, embossing heavily the bleached and twisted trunk and branches, so aged that there were but few green leaves thereon—a plumage of tender, crimson fire out of the heart of the dry wood. The perfume of the tree had now and again reached him, in the currents of the wind, over the wall, and he had wondered what might be behind it, and was now allowed to fill his arms with the flowers—flowers enough for all the old blue-china pots along the chimney-piece, making fête in the children's room. Was it some periodic moment in the expansion of soul within him, or mere trick of heat in the heavily-laden summer air? But the beauty of the thing struck home to him feverishly, and in dreams, all night, he loitered along a magic roadway of crimson flowers, which seemed to open ruddily in thick, fresh masses about his feet, and fill softly all the little hollows in the banks on either side. Always, afterwards, summer by summer, as the flowers came on, the blossom of the red hawthorn still seemed to him absolutely the reddest of all things; and the goodly crimson, still alive in the works of old Venetian masters, or old Flemish tapestries, called out always from afar the recollection of the flame in those perishing little petals, as it pulsed gradually out of them, kept long in the drawers of an old cabinet.

WALTER PATER

A Particular Garden

The garden has had to take care of itself under such circumstances, and if the house has been pushing it back in one place, it has wormed itself in at another, and queer little lawns with flower beds of old-fashioned, sweet-smelling plants have crept in where you least expect them. This particular garden has always seemed to me the ideal of what a garden should be. It is made to sit in, to smoke in, to think in, to do nothing in. A wavy, irregular lawn forbids the possibility of tennis, or any game that implies exertion or skill, and it is the home of sweet smells, bright colour, and chuckling birds. There are long borders of mignonette, wallflowers and hollyhocks, and many old-fashioned flowers, which are going the way of all old fashions. London pride, with its delicate spirals and star-like blossoms, and the red drooping velvet of love-lies-a-bleeding. The thump of tennis balls, the flying horrors of ring-goal, even the clash of croquet is tabooed in this sacred spot. Down below, indeed, beyond that thick privet hedge, you may find, if you wish, a smooth, well-kept piece of grass, where, even now—if we may judge from white figures that cross the little square, where a swinging iron gate seems to remonstrate hastily and ill-temperedly with those who leave these reflective shades for the glare and publicity of tennis—a game seems to be in progress. If you had exploring tendencies in your nature, and had you happened to find yourself, on the afternoon of which I propose to speak, in this delightful garden, you would sooner or later have wandered into a low-lying grassy basin, shut in on three sides by banks of bushy rose-trees. The faint, delicate smell of their pale fragrance would have led you there, or, perhaps, the light trickling of a fountain, now nearly summer dry.

E F BENSON

Monet's Garden at Giverny

Nature imitates art
Say painters philosophically
And Monet's garden at Giverny
Is approached through art,
Anticipated as an impression
By crowds who come
After sitting before

Les Nymphéas by Monet
In the Orangerie.
From Paris,
Where the mottled barks of maples
Face rows of chestnut trees,
They trek to Giverny
Hoping nature will imitate
Monet's elusive art.
They take train and taxi
Primed by preconceptions.

It is an illusion.
The Water Lily Studio
Is hung with reproductions
While the primary colours of the artist's house
Are fresh.
The gardens—
Clos Normand and Water Garden—
Are restorations.
What remains is the idea of Monet,
An impression of an Impressionist
(A label stuck on him
Like a red dot
In a commercial gallery).

In the Clos Normand
Flowers flaunt their colours,
Shining through the seasons:
Azaleas and irises,
Lilacs and larkspurs,
Lupins and lilies;
Hollyhocks, sunflowers,
Foxgloves and phlox;
Clematis and bellflowers,
Tulips and tamarisks,
Snapdragons, morning glories.
Words slide into silence
As colours proclaim their own praise.

In the Water Garden
Wistarias cling
To the Japanese Bridge.
There are ornaments of agapanthus

By the stream of water
That taps the Epte
As the Seine snakes by
Beds of fern,
Banks of rhododendron.
Bamboos cluster,
Willows weep,
Thalictrums lounge on the lawns.

These are not Monet's waterlilies
Floating on the water
Though his painted image
Is imprinted on them
Like a patent.
He painted an ideal,
A vision
Untouched by others.
The crowds who crush to share
The air of the flowers
Are unfocused in the vision.

Monet crossed a bridge
From colour to concept—
Cathedrals in his memory,
Cataracts in his eyes—
And saw peace in a place
Without people.
He watched waterlilies
And created the contours
Of a dream.

'I am good for nothing,'
Monet observed,
'Except painting and gardening.'
It will suffice.
One man in the morning,
The grandeur of a garden:
It will suffice
As an example,
An inspiration,
An impression
Of perfection.

Art does not imitate nature.
Art is the best part
Of human nature.

ALAN BOLD

SHARING_THE GARDEN

All Together

Dost thou not see the little plants, the little birds, the ants, the spiders, the bees working together to put in order their several parts of the universe?

MARCUS AURELIUS

If It Moves

If it moves slowly enough, step on it; if it doesn't, leave it—it'll probably kill something else.

ANON

A Noiseless Patient Spider

A noiseless patient spider,
I mark'd where on a little promontory it stood isolated,
Mark'd how to explore the vacant vast surrounding,
It launch'd forth filament, filament, filament, out of itself,
Ever unreeling them, ever tirelessly speeding them.

And you O my soul where you stand,
Surrounded, detached, in measureless oceans of space,
Ceaselessly musing, venturing, throwing, seeking the spheres to
    connect them,
Till the bridge you will need be form'd, till the ductile anchor hold,
Till the gossamer thread you fling catch somewhere, O my soul.

WALT WHITMAN

The Red Spider

One of the most troublesome insects is the active little mite called by gardeners the red spider (*A'carus telàrius*). This little pest breeds in the bark, and when first hatched it is so small as to be scarcely perceptible; particularly as it is of a pale green, nearly the colour of the under side of the leaf, to which it fixes itself, and there spins a web. As it gets older it becomes of a brownish red, and, having eight legs, it runs with the greatest rapidity. It is also furnished with a proboscis, with which it sucks the juices of the leaves, which wither and shrivel up; and thus the flowers and the fruit of the trees are both spoiled, as neither can attain perfection unless the sap that is to nourish them be first properly matured in the leaves. Tobacco smoke, and most of the other usual remedies against insects, have no effect on the red spider; and, though sprinkling it with very cold water will kill it, it is difficult to apply without injuring the plants. The best remedy is allowing plenty of air to pass through the [green] house.

JANE LOUDON

Earwig

You have more nicknames
than legs—some so strange, clipshears,
you'd think people give nicknames
to your nicknames.

Lord God, Saviour, Father,
your nicknames are
ingratiating flatteries.

Devil, Auld Nick, Clootie,
your nicknames
are shuddering familiarities.

I watch you, hornie-goloch,
trekking blindly across
the Gobi Desert of the floor.

Nickname the floor Life:
that's what I trek across.

But nobody ever
nicknamed me. I feel deprived.

Shall I call myself Earwig
and trek manfully on, seeking
the crumb of comfort,
the sighing, shining oasis?

NORMAN MacCAIG

Getting Rid of Earwigs

To clear your Garden of Earwigs, Mons. Gentil advises to get
Rams-horns, the Smell of which will tempt them to creep in,
which you must empty every Day, and so you will preserve your
Wall-Fruit.

PHILIP MILLER

Caterpillar

He stands on the suckers under his tail,
Stretches forward and puts down
his six legs. Then he brings up
the sucker under his tail, making a beautiful loop.

That's his way of walking. He makes
a row of upside-down U's
along the rib of a leaf. He is as green
as it.

NORMAN MacCAIG

To a Butterfly

I've watched you now a full half-hour,
Self-poised upon that yellow flower;
And, little Butterfly! indeed
I know not if you sleep or feed.
How motionless!—not frozen seas
More motionless; and then

What joy awaits you, when the breeze
Hath found you out among the trees,
And calls you forth again!

This plot of orchard ground is ours;
My trees they are, my sister's flowers;
Here rest your wings when they are weary,
Here lodge as in a sanctuary!
Come often to us, fear no wrong;
Sit near us on the bough!
We'll talk of sunshine and of song:
And summer days, when we were young;
Sweet childish days, that were as long
As twenty days are now.

WILLIAM WORDSWORTH

To A Butterfly In An Overgrown Garden

This butterfly to the flowerhead clings,
forming a new and fairer flower of wings.

You give up your own identity:
now, are you flower or butterfly?

It's in the nature of the pretty
to survive by mimicry.

I look down on you from above:
who gave the self away for love?

You look up at me from below
and use your wings to go.

If I see you in terms of me,
refresh me with your ambiguity.

VALERIE GILLIES

The Ladybird

Ladybird! Ladybird! Where art thou gone?
Ere the daisy was open or the rose it was spread
On the cabbage flower early thy scarlet wings shone,
I saw thee creep off to the tulip's bed.
Ladybird! Ladybird! Where art thou flown?
Thou wert here in the morning before the sun shone.

Just now up the bole o' the damson tree
You pass the gold lichen and got to the grey—
Ladybird! Ladybird! Where can you be?
You climb up the tulips and then fly away.
You crept up the flowers while I plucked them just now
And crept to the top and then flew from the flowers.
O sleep not so high as the damson tree bough,
But come from the dew i' the eldern tree bower.

Here's lavendar trees that would hide a lone mouse
And lavendar cotton wi' buttons o' gold,
And bushes o' lad's love as dry as a house,
Here's red pinks and daisies so sweet to behold.
Ladybird! Ladybird! Come to thy nest,
Thy gold bed's i' the rose o' the sweet brier tree,
Wi' rose coloured curtains to pleasure thee best;
Come, Ladybird, back to thy garden and me.

JOHN CLARE

The Grasshopper
TO MY NOBLE FRIEND, MR CHARLES COTTON

O thou that swing'st upon the waving hair
   Of some well-filléd oaten beard,
Drunk every night with a delicious tear
   Dropped thee from heaven, where now th'art reared;

The joys of earth and air are thine entire,
   That with thy feet and wings dost hop and fly;
And, when thy poppy works, thou dost retire
   To thy carved acorn-bed to lie.

Up with the day, the sun thou welcom'st then,
    Sport'st in the gilt plats of his beams,
And all these merry days mak'st merry men,
    Thyself, and melancholy streams.

But ah, the sickle! Golden ears are cropped;
    Ceres and Bacchus bid good night;
Sharp, frosty fingers all your flowers have topped,
    And what scythes spared, winds shave off quite.

Poor verdant fool, and now green ice! thy joys,
    Large and as lasting as thy perch of grass,
Bid us lay in 'gainst winter rain, and poise
    Their floods with an o'erflowing glass.

Thou best of men and friends! we will create
    A genuine summer in each other's breast,
And spite of this cold time and frozen fate,
    Thaw us a warm seat to our rest.

Our sacred hearths shall burn eternally,
    As vestal flames the North Wind, he
Shall strike his frost-stretched wings, dissolve, and fly
    This Etna in epitome.

Dropping December shall come weeping in,
    Bewail th' usurping of his reign:
But when in showers of old Greek we begin,
    Shall cry he hath his crown again!

Night, as clear Hesper, shall our tapers whip
    From the light casements where we play,
And the dark hag from her black mantle strip,
    And stick there everlasting day.

Thus richer than untempted kings are we,
    That, asking nothing, nothing need:
Though lord of all what seas embrace, yet he
    That wants himself is poor indeed.

RICHARD LOVELACE

Crickets

Crickets may be destroyed, like wasps, by phials half filled with beer, or any liquid, and set in their haunts, for, being always eager to drink, they will crowd in till the bottles are full.

GILBERT WHITE OF SELBORNE

Bees

The Pedigree of Honey
Does not concern the Bee—
A Clover, any time, to him,
Is Aristocracy—

To make a prairie it takes a clover and one bee,
One clover, and a bee,
And revery.
The revery alone will do,
If bees are few.

EMILY DICKINSON

The Honey Bees

For so work the honey bees,
Creatures that by a rule in nature teach
The act of order to a peopled kingdom.
They have a king, and officers of sort,
Where some like magistrates correct at home;
Others like merchants venture trade abroad;
Others like soldiers, armed in their stings.
Make boot upon the summer's velvet buds,
Which pillage they with merry march bring home
To the tent-royal of their emperor,
Who, busied in his majesty, surveys
The singing masons building roofs of gold,
The civil citizens kneading up the honey,

The poor mechanic porters crowding in
Their heavy burden sat his narrow gate,
The sad-ey'd justice, with his surly hum,
Delivering o'er to executors pale
The lazy yawning drone.

WILLIAM SHAKESPEARE

Bees

At the present time my garden is full of flowers, and the bees and
butterflies have come in corresponding numbers. I am sitting in front
of my house, with a book at my side, and wearing a large, yellow
straw hat. It has suddenly occurred to me that the colour of my hat
has made these bees and butterflies indifferent to my presence; and
that they regard me, sitting there so still and quiet, as so much corn,
or a certain flower known as golden rod.

Most of the bees are small and brown, and known as honey-bees,
and they are now filling their bags and thinking of a certain hive.
But the bee who fascinates me most is a large, black fellow with an
amber belt, who lives an independent life as a wanderer. He is much
larger than the common bee, and seeing him there makes me think of
a stallion among ponies. He has a much deeper voice than the brown
bee, and it comes low and deep, like a voice from the grave. He is so
heavy, and so clumsy in making love, that some of the weaker and
more slender flowers are bent double on their stalks.

W H DAVIES

The Bee's Song

Thousandz of thornz there be
On the Rozez where gozez
The Zebra of Zee:
Sleek, striped, and hairy,
The steed of the Fairy
Princess of Zee.

Heavy with blossomz be
The Rozez that growzez
In the thicketz of Zee.
Where grazez the Zebra,
Marked Abracadeeebra
Of the Princess of Zee.

And he nozez the poziez
Of the Rozez that growzez
So luvez'm and free,
With an eye, dark, and wary,
In search of a Fairy,
Whose Rozez he knowzez
Were not honied for he,
But to breathe a sweet incense
To solace the Princess
Of far-away Zee.

WALTER DE LA MARE

The Centipede

The centipede is not quite nice;
He lives in idleness and vice;
    He has a hundred legs.
He also has a hundred wives,
And each of these if she survives
    Has just a hundred eggs;
So that's the reason if you pick
Up any boulder, stone, or brick
    You nearly always find
A swarm of centipedes concealed;
They scatter far across the field,
    But *one* remains behind.
And you may reckon then, my son,
That not alone that luckless one
    Lies pitiful and torn,
But millions more of either sex—
100 multiplied by X—
    Will never now be born;
I dare say it will make you sick,

But so does all Arithmetic.
The gardener says, I ought to add,
The centipede is not so bad;
    He rather *likes* the brutes.
The millipede is what he loathes;
He uses wild bucolic oaths
    Because it eats his roots;
And every gardener is agreed
That if you see a centipede
    Conversing with a milli—
On one of them you drop a stone,
The other one you leave alone—
    I think that's rather silly;
They may be right, but what I say
Is 'Can one stand about all day
    And *count* the creature's legs?'
It has too many any way,
And any moment it may lay
    Another hundred eggs!
So if I see a thing like *this*
I murmur 'Without prejudice,'
    And knock it on the head;
And if I see a thing like *that*
I take a brick and squash it flat;
    In either case it's dead.

GUY BOAS

Worms

In their native soil, worms are so careful and so gentle. Under the apple trees in the garden the first flakes of blossom are lying; and, after dark, when the dew is falling, and condensing on the white petals, the worms move up their galleries from the lower earth and put out their heads and feel the night air. They listen—not with ears, but with their entire bodies, which are sensitive to light and to all ground vibration. Then, feeling that it is safe, one after another begins to move out of its tunnel, and with eager pointed head, to search for petals of fallen apple-blossom. When a petal is found, it is taken in the worm's mouth and the worm withdraws into its tunnel, and leaves the petal outside the hole. Then the worm moves out again in another direction, casting about until it finds another flake. This, too, is taken to the entrance of the tunnel...

When the worm has, and so carefully, gathered about a dozen petals at the mouth of its tunnel, it picks them up in its mouth, one after the other, and then goes down into the darkness and eats them. Thus the night-wanderer turns blossom into the finest soil, or humus, which feeds the roots of the tree once more. Worms are soil-makers; and their galleries and tunnels act as drains to the top-soil. They are poets, choosing at their annual spring festival the choicest food and converting it, after much enjoyment, into food for the trees again. Like poets, they are the natural priests of the earth.

HENRY WILLIAMSON

Earth-Worms

Lands that are subject to frequent inundations are always poor; and probably the reason may be because the worms are drowned. The most insignificant insects and reptiles are of much more consequence, and have much more influence in the economy of Nature, than the incurious are aware of; and are mighty in their effect, from their minuteness, which renders them less an object of attention; and from their numbers and fecundity. Earth-worms, though in appearance a small and despicable link in the chain of Nature, yet, if lost, would make a lamentable chasm. For, to say nothing of half the birds, and some quadrupeds which are almost entirely supported by them, worms seems to be the great promoters of vegetation, which would proceed but lamely without them, by boring, perforating, and loosening the soil, and rendering it pervious to rains and the fibres of plants, by drawing straws and stalks of leaves and twigs into it; and, most of all, by throwing up such infinite numbers of lumps of earth called worm-casts, which, being their excrement, is a fine manure for grain and grass. Worms probably provide new soil for hills and slopes where the rain washes the earth away; and they affect slopes, probably to avoid being flooded. Gardeners and farmers express their detestation of worms; the former because they render their walks unsightly, and make them much work: and the latter because, as they think, worms eat their green corn. But these men would find that the earth without worms would soon become cold, hard-bound, and void of fermentation; and consequently steril: and besides, in favour of worms, it should be hinted that green corn,

plants, and flowers, are not so much injured by them as by many
species of *coleoptera* (scarabs), and *tipulæ* (long-legs) in their larva, or
grub-state; and by unnoticed myriads of small shell-less snails, called
slugs, which silently and imperceptibly make amazing havoc in the
field and garden.

These hints we think proper to throw out in order to set the
inquisitive and discerning to work.

A good monography of worms would afford much entertainment
and information at the same time, and would open a large and new
field in natural history. Worms work most in the spring; but by no
means lie torpid in the dead months; are out every mild night in the
winter, as any person may be convinced that will take the pains to
examine his grass-plots with a candle; are hermaphrodites, and much
addicted to venery, and consequently very prolific.

GILBERT WHITE OF SELBORNE

Slug

On looking for the word Slug in the *Penny Cyclopædia* you will find
yourself referred to Limax, and under that head you will find a figure
very nearly resembling the creature you are seeking for, though it
differs in colour; as it is called Arìon rùfa, or the red slug, while the
creature you saw was the black slug, called Arìon àter; and if you
have the courage to examine the living animal you will find it very
curiously formed. Its back is covered with a black ribbed skin, and
on the upper part it bears a shield, which consists of a piece of bone,
the only one in the slug's body, covered with skin; the shield being
designed to protect the air-hole through which the creature breathes.
What we are accustomed to call its horns are, in fact, tentacula or
feelers, which the creature has the power of drawing into its body
or pushing out at pleasure, and which are gifted with an exquisitely
fine sense of touch. The long shining line with which the creature
marked its path is the slime which proceeds from its body, and with
which it is enabled to glide smoothly over sand or gravel that would
otherwise injure it. I have said more on this subject than I should
otherwise have done, because I wish to point out to you that even
a creature so humble and so despicable as a slug, is as curiously
and wonderfully made, and displays the power and wisdom of its
Creator, as decidedly, as the noblest and most beautiful animal.

JANE LOUDON

Black Snail

'Tis evening, the black snail has got on his track,
And gone to its nest is the wren;—
And the packman snail too, with his home on his back,
Clings on the bowed bents like a wen.

JOHN CLARE

The Snail

We should learn from the snail: it has devised a home that is both
exquisite and functional.

FRANK LLOYD WRIGHT

Hedgehog

Some nocturnal blackness, mothy and warm,
When the hedgehog travels furtively over the lawn.

THOMAS HARDY

Toad

Stop looking like a purse. How could a purse
squeeze under the rickety door and sit,
full of satisfaction, in a man's house?

You clamber towards me on your four corners—
right hand, left foot, left hand, right foot.

I love you for being a toad,
for crawling like a Japanese wrestler,
and for not being frightened.

I put you in my purse hand, not shutting it,
and set you down outside directly under
every star.

A jewel in your head? Toad,
you've put one in mine,
a tiny radiance in a dark place.

NORMAN MacCAIG

The Lincolnshire Bagpipes

Multitude of frogs croaking tonight which they call here the Lincoln-
shire bagpipes and is a sign of rain.

DION CLAYTON CALTHORP

Cats

In my little Chelsea garden the walls were low and allowed a
maximum of sunlight. However, the walls were also broad and
supported a maximum of cats. It was soon evident that the boundary
wall was the recognised promenade for all the cats of Chelsea...it was
a sort of feline Piccadilly. Every day, towards the hour of dusk, dark
figures would emerge from neighbouring scullery windows, stretch,
yawn, and take a sudden bound on to this wall. Having bounded,
they would proceed to saunter, with assumed nonchalance, in the
direction of my little piece of wall.

As the shadows deepened, more and more of the dark figures
emerged. They hopped delicately from the branches of trees. They
appeared from sombre doorways, their eyes catching the last glint
of the dying sun. Like tiny dots, they were seen in the distance, as
though they had fallen from the clouds. And soon the whole wall
was crowned with a stealthy procession of arched backs and feathery
tails, passing to and fro, in a strange and ghostly saraband...

I found there was only one way to get rid of them...the remedy was
treacle. Small pools of treacle, carefully poured on to the top of the
wall, and renewed once a week. My original intention had been to
scare the cats away altogether. They are the daintiest creatures, and
I hoped that when they found themselves stepping into the sticky
treacle they would shake their paws, sniff, and go back home. They
would think me a common brute, but I could not help that.

However, they did not do what I expected them to do. (No cat ever does.) They approached my wall, stepped in the treacle, paused a moment in astonishment, and then hopped away to a little distance to lick their paws. For one reason or another, they no longer jumped down on to my flower-beds.

BEVERLEY NICHOLS

The Value of Weeds

The weeds keep the earth moist, and prevent the radiation of heat, and how much they do so most of us can see by observing the plantains on our lawns. I am not fond of plantains on lawns, and get rid of them; but some will remain, and on them I have often noticed that in a slight hoar-frost no hoar-frost is formed on the plantains; the broad leaves flying flat on the ground keep in the earth-heat.

CANON HENRY ELLACOMBE

A Weed

What is a weed? A plant whose virtues have not been discovered.

RALPH WALDO EMERSON

A Weed

A weed is but a good plant in the wrong place.

CANON HENRY ELLACOMBE

Weeds

There is perhaps a sort of sacredness about them [weeds]. Perhaps if we could penetrate Nature's secrets we should find that what we call weeds are more essential to the well-being of the world, than the most precious fruit or grain.

NATHANIEL HAWTHORNE

Weeds

For everything I felt a love
The weeds below, the birds above
And weeds that bloomed in Summer's hours
I thought they should be reckoned flowers.
They made a garden free for all
And so I loved them great and small
...Until I even danced for joy
A happy and a lonely boy.

JOHN CLARE

Couch Grasse or Dogs Grasse

It creepeth in the ground hither and thither with long white roots ioynted at certaine distances, having a pleasant sweet tast...great labour must be taken before it can be destroyed, each piece being apt to grow, and every way to dilate itself.

JOHN GERARDE

Couch Grass

Couch-grass is a no-nonsense grass.
Cuts tubes through clay, tilts bricks,
    Advances in phalanxes,
        Spears docks.

Quitch-grass is a live-wire grass.
Half-a-chance, soil's quick with it:
   Mesh your hand down in a mass,
     —Taut net.

Couch-grass is a rat-race grass.
Uses its nous-sweet smile, bear-hug
   —Takes over the whole patch,
     Top dog.

Quitch-grass is a Realpolitik grass.
If you want to get on, act tough.
   Elbow your way through! Lash out!
     The rough stuff!

DEREK BOWMAN

Wet and Wilderness

What would the world be, once bereft
Of wet and wilderness? Let them be left,
O let them be left, wildness and wet;
Long live the weeds and the wilderness yet.

GERALD MANLEY HOPKINS

TUSSIE-MUSSIE

A Tussie-Mussie

There be some flowers make a delicious Tussie-Mussie or Nosegay both for sight and smell.

JOHN PARKINSON

The Snowdrop

The snowdrop is a very star of hope in a season of wreck and decay, the one bright link between the perishing good of the past and the better which has not yet begun to follow.

FORBES WATSON

Snowdrops in March

Curious that these long-overdue February flowers
Should come almost unexpected to our
Remote world: and they suspensive in cold and light
Now remain even in their proper powers

Like a legend, dreamt of, not hoped on;
Nor for us, these, delicate, of perfect leaf
And petal, but secret hold
For other Springs their promissory note.

GEORGE BRUCE

Daffodils

...daffodils
That come before the swallow dares, and take
The winds of March with beauty; violets dim,
But sweeter than the lids of Juno's eyes
Or Cytherea's breath; pale prime-roses,

That die unmarried, ere they can behold
Bright Phoebus in his strength,—a malady
Most incident to maids; bold oxlips and
The crown imperial; lilies of all kinds,
The flower-de-luce being one.

WILLIAM SHAKESPEARE

Through Primrose Tufts

Through primrose tufts, in that green bower,
The periwinkle trailed its wreaths;
And 'tis my faith that every flower
Enjoys the air it breathes.

WILLIAM WORDSWORTH

Along the Blushing Borders

Along the blushing borders, bright with dew,
And on yon mingled wilderness of flowers,
Fair-handed Spring unbosoms every grace;
Throws out the snowdrop, and the crocus first;
The daisy, primrose, violet darkly blue,
And polyanthus of unnumbered dyes;
The yellow wall-flower stained with iron brown;
And lavish stock that scents the garden round:
From the soft wing of vernal breezes shed,
Anemonies; auriculas, enriched
With shining meal o'er all their velvet leaves;
And full ranunculas, of glowing red.
Then comes the tulip-race, where Beauty plays
Her idle freaks; from family diffused
To family, as flies the father-dust,
The varied colours run; and, while they break
On the charmed eye, th' exultant florist marks,
With secret pride, the wonders of his hand,
No gradual bloom is wanting; from the bud,
First-born of Spring, to Summer's musky tribes:
Nor hyacinths, deep-purpled; nor jonquils,
Of potent fragrance; nor narcissus fair,

As o'er the fabled fountain hanging still;
Nor broad carnations, nor gay-spotted pinks;
Nor, showered from every bush, the damask-rose
Infinite numbers, delicacies, smells,
With hues on hues expression cannot paint,
The breath of Nature, and her endless bloom.

JAMES THOMSON

Tulips

The tulips to delight your eyes
With glorious garments, rich and new,
Like the rich glutton some are dight
In Tyrian-purple and fine white;
And in bright crimson others shine
Impal'd with white and greydeline:
The meanest here you can behold,
Is cloth'd in scarlet, lac'd with gold.
But then the queen of all delight
Wears greydeline, scarlet and white:
So interwov'n and so plac'd,
That all the others are disgrac'd
When she appears and doth impart
Her native beauties, shaming art.

JOHN REA

Tulips

Erect and slender, sculptured in green bronze,
Arrogant as hidalgos of Castile,
Proudest of all the Sun's Spring myrmidons,
They wait his lifted standard, immobile.

Flanked haughtily by chevroned leaves, they rise,
Calm-sheathed in confident expectancy,
Their close-furled banners spiring towards the skies
In ceremonial pledge of fealty.

Rank upon formal rank, they stand serene,
Stately, aloof, yet gracious; every one
Austere in patina of sombre green
Till flares the royal summons of the Sun

Then down the ranks, steadfast in sculptured grace,
Saluting pennons splendidly unfold,
The august homage of a lordly race,
Blazoned in scarlet copper, black, and gold.

MICHAEL SCOT

A Toolip

There is lately a *Flower* (shal I call it so? in courtesie I will tearme
it so, though it deserve not the appellation) a *Toolip*, which hath
engrafted the love and affections of most people unto it; and what
is this Toolip? a well complexion'd stink, an ill favour wrapt up in
pleasant colours; as for the use thereof in *Physick*, no *Physitian* hath
honoured it yet with the mention, nor with a *Greek*, or Latin name,
so inconsiderable hath it hitherto been accompted; and yet this is
that which filleth all Gardens, hundred of pounds being given for
the root thereof, whilst I the *Rose*, am neglected and contemned, and
conceived beneath the honour of noble hands, and fit only to grow in
the gardens of Yeomen. I trust the remainder to your apprehensions,
to make out that which grief for such undeserved injuries will not
suffer me to expresse.

THOMAS FULLER

How the Wallflower Came First and Why So Called

Why this flower is now called so,
List' sweet maids, and you shall know,
Understand, this firstling was
Once a brisk and bonny lass,
Kept as close as Danae was:
Who a sprightly springall loved,

And to have it full proved,
Up she got upon a wall,
'Tempting down to slide withall:
But the silken twist untied,
So she fell, and bruis'd, she died.
Love, in pity of the deed,
And her loving-luckless speed,
Turned her to this plant, we call
Now, The Flower of the Wall.

ROBERT HERRICK

Flower in the Crannied Wall

Flower in the crannied wall,
I pluck you out of the crannies,
I hold you here, root and all, in my hand,
Little flower—but *if* I could understand
What you are, root and all, and all in all,
I should know what God and Man is.

ALFRED, LORD TENNYSON

I Remember

I remember, I remember,
The roses, red and white,
The vi'lets and the lily-cups,
Those flowers made of light!
The lilacs where the robin built,
And where my brother set
The laburnum on his birthday,—
The tree is living yet!

THOMAS HOOD

When Lilacs Last in the Dooryard Bloom'd

When lilacs last in the dooryard bloom'd,
And the great star early droop'd in the western sky in the night,
I mourn'd, and yet shall mourn with ever-returning spring.

Ever-returning spring, trinity sure to me you bring,
Lilac blooming perennial and drooping star in the west,
And thought of him I love.

O powerful western fallen star!
O shaded of night–O moody, tearful night!
O great star disappear'd–O the black murk that hides the star!
O cruel hands that hold me powerless–O helpless soul of me!
O harsh surrounding cloud that will not free my soul.

In the dooryard fronting an old farm-house near the white-wash'd
    palings,
Stands the lilac-bush tall-growing with heart-shaped leaves of rich
    green,
With many a pointed blossom rising delicate, with the perfume
    strong I love,
With every leaf a miracle–and from this bush in the dooryard,
With delicate-color'd blossoms and heart-shaped leaves of rich
    green,
A sprig with its flower I break.

WALT WHITMAN

Lilac Blossoms

We mark the playing-time of sun and rain,
Until the rain too heavily upon us
Leans, and the sun stamps down upon our lustres,
And then our trees stand in their greennesses
No different from the privets in the hedges,
And we who made a pleasaunce at the door-step,
And, whether by the ash-heap or the spring-well
Growing, were ever fresh and ever radiant,

And fragrant more than grass is—
We, we are gone without a word that praised us—
You did not know how short the playing-time!

PADRAIC COLUM

Summer-Sweet

Honey-sweet, sweet as honey smell the lilies,
    Little lilies of the gold in a ring;
Little censers of pale gold are the lilies,
    That the wind, sweet and sunny, sets a-swing.

Smell the rose, sweet of sweets, all a-blowing!
    Hear the cuckoo call in dreams, low and sweet!
Like a very John-a-Dreams coming, going.
    There's honey in the grass at our feet.

There's honey in the leaf and the blossom,
    And honey in the night and the day,
And honey-sweet the heart in Love's bosom,
    And honey-sweet the words Love will say.

KATHERINE TYNAN

Lily-Lowe

O orange tiger-lily, burnan bricht,
swung lantern at the end o the sun's licht,
your caunel-stamens' drippan yella ase
dazzles the bummers wi its dusty haze
and your silk petals' incandescent flare,
like het, fresh wax, sae mells wi the deep air
o hinnied Simmer, that I canna tell
jist whaur the blue lift rings the rim o your bell.

MAURICE LINDSAY

High Midsummer

Soon will the high midsummer pomps come on,
Soon will the musk carnations break and swell,
Soon shall we have gold-dusted snapdragon,
Sweet-William with his homely cottage smell,
And stocks in fragrant blow;
Roses that down the alleys shine afar,
And open jasmine-muffled lattices,
And groups under the dreaming garden-trees,
And the full moon and the white evening star.

MATTHEW ARNOLD

Roses

The Plant of Roses, though it be a shrub full of prickles, yet it had been more fit and convenient to have placed it with the most glorious floures of the world, than to inset the same here among base and thorny shrubs: for the Rose doth deserve the chief and prime place among all floures whatsoever; being...esteemed for his beauty, vertues, and his fragrant and odoriferous smell.

JOHN GERARDE

Sweet is the Rose

SWEET is the rose, but grows upon a brere;
Sweet is the juniper, but sharp his bough;
Sweet is the eglantine, but pricketh near;
Sweet is the fir-bloom, but his branches rough;
Sweet is the cypress, but his rind is tough;
Sweet is the nut, but bitter is his pill;
Sweet is the broom-flower, but yet sour enough;
And sweet is moly, but his root is ill.
So every sweet with sour is tempered still,
That maketh it be coveted the more;
For easy things, that may be got at will,
Most sorts of men do set but little store.

Why then should I account of little pain,
That endless pleasure shall unto me gain?

EDMUND SPENSER

Promise

I grew a rose within a garden fair,
And, tending it with more than loving care,
I thought how, with the glory of its bloom,
I should the darkness of my life illume;
And, watching, ever smiled to see the lusty bud
Drink freely in the summer sun to tint its blood.

My rose began to open, and its hue
Was sweet to me as to it sun and dew;
I watched it taking on its ruddy flame
Until the day of perfect blooming came,
Then hasted I with smiles to find it blushing red–
Too late! Some thoughtless child had plucked my
    rose and fled!

PAUL LAURENCE DUNBAR

Rock Roses

At breakfast time on summer days
Our rockery is all ablaze
With mingled rose and mauve and white
To dazzle and enchant the sight;
It is not trimmed with tidy care
And little labels here and there
To point some almost hidden treasure
But heaped with overflowing measure
Of purple catmint, saxifrages,
Cerastium in snowy stages,
While gorgeous in the sunlight glows
The colour of the Alpine rose,
The deepest, rarest pink that blesses
Only these flowers and silken dresses.
Then when the sun has mounted high

The rosy petals fall and die
Until the brilliant morning scene
In quiet mauve and white and green,
At eventide to fade away
Into a softly shaded grey.
But with the light of morning, lo!
Triumphant the rock roses glow:
New every day they tell their story
Of radiance and morning glory.

MARGARET LODGE

Sweetpeas

Here are sweet-peas, on tip-toe for a flight
With wings of gentle flush o'er delicate white,
And taper fingers catching at all things,
To bind them all about with tiny rings.

JOHN KEATS

The Names of Flowers

Their names were nymphs, and they were
    nymphs indeed,
A whole mythology from pinch of seed.
Nemesia and Viscaria, and that
Blue-as-the-butterfly Phacelia;
Love-in-mist Nigella, whose strong brat
Appears unwanted like a very weed;
Nemōphila,—I knew a little boy
Who called his doll Nemōphilia, for joy
In that Greek word he fitted to a toy;
But there's no end within a list that sheds
Petals on summer, seeds on autumn beds,
A list elaborate as chime of bells
Known to the ringer in the composite peal
Where difficult art must difficult skill conceal,
Each separately used but woven in their time
To make the melody of perfect chime
Over the listening landscape richly rolled;

So does the gardener choose a list to hold
Sweet Sultan and Sweet Alyssum that smells
Of sea-clifs and short turf
Where move the cropping sheep
And sea-gulls waver sprinkled round the steep
Crags that descend into the constant surf;
A list of mignonette and marigold
And other pretty things,
But lest you be romancefully inclined
Thinking that beauty unattended springs
All jilly-jolly from your scatterings,
Let dull instruction here remind
That mignonette is tricky, and demands
Firm soil, and lime, to follow your commands,
Else failure comes, and shows a barren space
Where you had looked for small but scented spires.

V SACKVILLE-WEST

The Flowers of Her Garden

Prim little scholars are the flowers of her garden,
    Trained to stand in rows, and asking if they please.
I might love them well but for loving more the wild ones:
    O my wild ones! they tell me more than these.
You, my wild one, you tell of honied field-rose,
    Violet, blushing eglantine in life; and even as they,
They by the wayside are earnest of your goodness,
    You are of life's, on the banks that line the way.

Peering at her chamber the white crowns the red rose,
    Jasmine winds the porch with stars two and three.
Parted is the window; she sleeps; the starry jasmine
    Breathes a falling breath that carries thoughts of me.
Sweeter unpossessed, have I said of her my sweetest?
    Not while she sleeps: while she sleeps the jasmine breathes,
Luring her to love; she sleeps; the starry jasmine
    Bears me to her pillow under white rose-wreaths.

Yellow with birdsfoot-trefoil are the grass-glades;
    Yellow with cinquefoil of the dew-grey leaf;

Yellow with stonecrop; the moss-mounds are yellow
   Blue-necked the wheat sways, yellowing to the sheaf.
Green-yellow bursts from the copse the laughing yaffle;
   Sharp as a sickle is the edge of shade and shine:
Earth in her heart laughs looking at the heavens,
   Thinking of the harvest: I look and think of mine.

     *   *   *   *   *

Could I find a place to be alone with heaven,
   I would speak my heart out: heaven is my need.
Every woodland tree is flushing like the dogwood,
   Flashing like the whitebeam, swaying like the reed.
Flushing like the dogwood crimson in October;
   Streaming like the flag-reed South-West blown;
Flashing as in gusts the sudden-lighted whitebeam:
   All seems to know what is for heaven alone.

                GEORGE MEREDITH

Bring Hither the Pink and Purple Columbine

Bring hither the Pink and purple Columbine,
    With gillyflowers:
Bring Coronation, and Sops in wine,
    Worn of paramours.
Strew me the ground with Daffadowndillies,
And cowslips, and Kingcups, and loved lilies:
    The pretty Pawnce,
    And the Chevisaunce,
Shall match with the fair flower Delice.

                EDMUND SPENSER

Rosemary

There's rosemary, that's for remembrance;
pray you, love, remember; and there is pansies,
that's for thoughts.

There's fennel for you, and columbines;
there's rue for you; and here's some for me;
we may call it herb of grace o' Sundays; oh,
you must wear your rue with a difference.
There's a daisy; I would give you some
violets, but they withered all when my father
died; they say he made a good end...

WILLIAM SHAKESPEARE

The Chrysanthemum Show

Here's Abbey Way: here are the rooms
   Where they held the chrysanthemum show—
Leaves like talons of greenfire, blooms
Of a barbarous frenzy, red, flame, bronze—
And a schoolboy walked in the furnace once,
   Thirty years ago.

You might have thought, had you seen him that day
   Mooching from stall to stall,
It was wasted on him—the prize array
Of flowers with their resinous, caustic tang,
Their colours that royally boomed and rang
   Like gongs in the pitchpine hall.

Any tongue could scorch him; even hope tease
   As if it dissembled a leer:
   Like smouldering fuse, anxieties
Blindwormed his breast. How should one feel,
Consuming in youth's slow ordeal,
   What flashes from flower to flower?

Yet something did touch him then, at the quick,
   Like a premature memory prising
Through flesh. Those blooms with the bonfire reek
And the flaming of ruby, copper, gold—
There boyhood's sun foretold, retold
   A full gamut of setting and rising.

Something touched him. Always the scene
   Was to haunt his memory—
Not haunt—come alive there, as if what had been
But a flowery idea took flesh in the womb
Of his solitude, rayed out a rare, real bloom.
   I know, for I was he.

And today, when I see chrysanthemums,
   I half envy that boy
For whom they spoke as muffled drums
Darkly messaging, 'All decays;
But youth's brief agony can blaze
   Into a posthumous joy.'

C DAY LEWIS

Bright as the Silvery Plume

Bright as the silvery plume, or pearly shell,
The snow-white rose or lily's virgin bell,
The fair helleborus attractive shone,
Warmed every sage and every shepherd won.

ERASMUS DARWIN

I Have Loved Flowers That Fade

I have loved flowers that fade,
Within whose magic tents
Rich hues have marriage made
With sweet unmemoried scents:
A honeymoon delight,—
A joy of love at sight,
That ages in an hour:—
My song be like a flower!

I have loved airs, that die
Before their charm is writ
Along a liquid sky
Trembling to welcome it.

Notes, that with pulse of fire
Proclaim the spirit's desire,
Then die, and are nowhere:—
My song be like an air!

Die, song, die like a breath,
And wither as a bloom:
Fear not a flowery death,
Dread not an airy tomb!
Fly with delight, fly hence!
'Twas thine love's tender sense
To feast; now on thy bier
Beauty shall shed a tear.

ROBERT BRIDGES

The Value of Trees

I never before knew the value of trees. My house is entirely em-
bosomed in high plane trees, with good grass below, and under
them, I breakfast, dine, write, read and receive my company under
them. What would I not give that the trees planted nearest round the
house at Monticello were full grown?

THOMAS JEFFERSON

Laburnums

Over old walls the Laburnums
        hang cones of fire;
Laburnums that grow out of old
        mould in old gardens:

Old maids and old men who have savings or pensions
    have
Shuttered themselves in the pales of old gardens.

The gardens grow wild; out of their mould the Laburnums
Draw cones of fire.

And we, who've no lindens, no palms, no cedars of
   Lebanon,
Rejoice you have gardens with mould, old men and old
   maids:

The bare and the dusty streets have now the Laburnums,
Have now cones of fire!

PADRAIC COLUM

A Health to the Trees

Wassaile the trees that they may beare
You many a plum and many a peare:
For more or less fruit they will bring,
As you do give them wassailing.

ROBERT HERRICK

The Apple Tree

Let there be Light!
In pink and white
The apple tree blooms for our delight.
In pink and white,
Its shout unheard,
The Logos itself, the Creative Word,
Bursts from nothing; and all is stirred.
It blooms and blows and shrivels to fall
Down on the earth in a pink-white pall,
Withered? But look at each little green ball,
Crowned like a globe in the hand of God,
Each little globe on a shortening rod;
Soon to be rosy and well bestowed,
A cosmos now where the blossoms glowed
Constellated around the tree,
A cone that lifts to infinity.
Each rosy globe is as red as Mars;
And all the tree is a branch of stars.
What can we say but, 'Glory be!'
When God breaks out in an apple tree?

OLIVER ST JOHN GOGARTY

A Tree

I care not how men trace their ancestry,
To ape or Adam; let them please their whim;
But I in June am midway to believe
A tree among my far progenitors,
Such sympathy is mine with all the race,
Such mutual recognition vaguely sweet
There is between us. Surely there are times
When they consent to own me of their kin,
And condescend to me, and call me cousin,
Murmuring faint lullabies of eldest time,
Forgotten, and yet dumbly felt with thrills
Moving the lips, though fruitless of the words.
And I have many a life-long leafy friend,
Never estranged nor careful of my soul,
That knows I hate the axe, and welcomes me
Within his tent as if I were a bird,
Or other free companion of the earth,
Yet undegenerate to the shifts of men.

J R LOWELL

Last Lauch

The Minister said it wald dee,
the cypress buss I plantit.
But the buss grew til a tree,
naething dauntit.

It's growan, stark and heich,
derk and straucht and sinister,
kirkyairdie-like and dreich.
But whaur's the Minister?

DOUGLAS YOUNG

FIGURES IN THE GARDEN

The Book of Life

Lord Illingworth: The book of Life begins with a man and a woman
in a Garden.

Mrs Allonby: It ends with Revelations.

OSCAR WILDE

The Garden of Eden

In the Garden of Eden sat Adam,
Disporting himself with his madam.
    She was filled with elation,
    For in all of creation
There was only one man—and she had'm.

ANON

The Eye of Day

   And Zephirus and Flora gentilly
Yaf to the floures, softe and tenderly,
Hir swote breth, and made hem for to sprede,
As god and goddesse of the floury mede;
Til at the laste a larke song above:
'I see,' quod she, 'the mighty god of love!
Lo! yond he cometh, I see his winges sprede!'
Tho gan I loken enderlong the mede,
In which me thoghte I mighte, day by day,
Dwellen alwey, the joly month of May,
Withouten sleep, withouten mete or drinke.
A-dounful softely I gan to sinke;
And, leninge on myn elbowe and my syde,
The longe day I shoop me for to abyde
For nothing elles, and I shal nat lye,
But for to loke upon the dayesye,

That wel by reson men hit calle may
The 'dayesye' or elles the 'ye of day,'
The emperice and flour of floures alle.

GEOFFREY CHAUCER

A Garden Fair

Bewailing in my chamber thus allone,
   Despeired of all joye and remedye,
For-tiret of my thought and wo-begone,
   And to the wyndow gan I walk in hye,
To see the warld and folk that went forbye,
   As for the tyme though I of mirthis fude
   Mycht have no more, to luke it did me gude.

Now was there maid fast by the Touris wall
   A gardyn faire, and in the corneris set
Ane herbere grene, with wandis long and small
   Railit about, and so with treis set
Was all the place, and hawthorn hegis knet,
   That lyf was not walkyng there forbye,
   That myght within scarce any wight aspye.

So thick the beuis and the leves grene
   Beschadit all the allyes that there were,
And myddis every herbere mycht be sene
   The scharpe grene suete jenepere,
Growing so fair with branchis here and there,
   That, as it semyt to a lyf without,
   The bewis spred the herbere all about.

And on the smale grene twistis sat
   The lytil suete nyghtingale, and song
So loud and clere, the ympnis consecrat
   Of luvis use, now soft now lowd among,
That all the gardynis and the wallis rong
   Ryght of thaire song, and on the copill next
   Of thaire suete armony, and lo the text:
       *   *   *   *   *

And therewith kest I doun myn eye ageyne,
   Quhare as I saw walkyng under the Toure,
Full secretely, new cumyn hir to pleyne,
   The fairest or the freschest younge floure
That ever I sawe, methought, before that houre,
   For quhich sodayne abate, anon astert
   The blude of all my body to my hert.

And though I stood abaisit tho a lyte,
   No wonder was; for quhy? my wittis all
Were so oercome with plesance and delyte,
   Only through latting of myn eyen fall,
That sudaynly my hert become hir thrall,
   For ever of free wyll, for of manace
   There was no takyn in her suete face.

And in my hede I drew rycht hastily,
   And eft sones I lent it out ageyne.
And saw hir walk that verray womanly,
   With no wight mo, but only women tueyne,
Than gan I studye in myself and seyne,
   Ah! suete, are ye a warldly creature,
   Or hevinly thing in likeness of nature?

Or are ye god Cupidis owin princesse?
   And cumyn are to louse me out of band,
Or are ye veray Nature the goddesse,
   That have depayntit with your hevinly hand
This garden full of flouris, as they stand?
   Quhat sall I think, allace! quhat reverence
   Sall I minister to your excellence.

Giff ye a goddesse be, and that ye like
   To do me payne, I may it not astert;
Giff ye be warldly wight, that dooth me sike,
   Quhy lest God mak you so, my derest hert,
To do a sely prisoner thus smert,
   That lufis you all, and wote of nought but wo?
   And, therefor, merci, suete! sen it is so.

KING JAMES I OF SCOTLAND

To A Lady

Sweet rois of vertew and of gentilness,
Delytsum lily of everie lustynes,
   Richest in bontie and in bewtie clear,
   And everie vertew that is wenit dear,
Except onlie that ye are mercyless.

Into your garth this day I did persew;
There saw I flowris that fresche were of hew;
   Baith quhyte and reid most lusty were to seyne,
   And halesome herbis upon stalkis greene;
Yet leaf nor flowr find could I nane of rew.

I doubt that Merche, with his cauld blastis keyne,
Has slain this gentil herb, that I of mene;
   Quhois piteous death does to my heart sic paine
   That I would make to plant his root againe,—
So confortand his levis unto me bene.

WILLIAM DUNBAR

There Is a Garden in Her Face

There is a garden in her face,
Where roses and white lilies grow,
A heavenly paradise is that place,
Wherein all pleasant fruits do flow.
There cherries grow, which none may buy
Till 'Cherry ripe' themselves do cry.

Those cherries fairly do enclose
Of orient pearl a double row,
Which when her lovely laughter shows,
They look like rosebuds filled with snow.
Yet them nor peer nor prince can buy,
Till 'Cherry ripe' themselves do cry.

Her eyes like angels watch them still;
Her brows like bended bows do stand,

Threatening with piercing frowns to kill
All that attempt with eye or hand
Those sacred cherries to come nigh,
Till 'Cherry ripe!' themeselves do cry.

THOMAS CAMPION

Say, Crimson Rose

SAY, crimson rose and dainty daffodil,
  With violet blue,
Since you have seen the beauty of my saint,
  And eke her view,
Did not her sight (fair sight!) you lovely fill
  With sweet delight
Of goddess' grace and angel's sacred taint
  In fine, most bright?

Say, golden primrose, sanguine cowslip fair,
  With pink most fine,
Since you beheld the visage of my dear,
  And eyes divine,
Did not her globy front and glistering hair,
  With cheeks most sweet,
So gloriously like damask flowers appear,
  The gods to greet?

Say, snow-white lily, speckled gilly-flower,
  With daisy gay,
Since you have viewed the queen of my desire
  In brave array,
Did not her ivory paps, fair Venus' bower,
  With heavenly glee,
Of Juno's grace, conjure you to require
  Her face to see?

Say rose, say daffodil, and violet blue,
  With primrose fair,
Since you have seen my nymph's sweet dainty face
  And gesture rare,
Did not (bright cowslip, bloomy pink) her view

(White lily) shine
(Ah, gilly-flowers and daisy!) with a grace
Like stars divine?

JOHN REYNOLDS

A Well-Wishing to a Place of Pleasure

SEE that building, which, when my mistress living,
    Was pleasure's essence;
See how it droopeth, and how nakedly it looketh
    Without her presence;
Hark how the hollow wind doth blow
    And seems to murmur
    In every corner
For her being absent, from which doth chiefly grow
The cause that I do now this grief and sorrow show.

See that garden, where oft I had reward in
    For my true love;
See the places, where I enjoyed those graces
    The gods might move;
Oft in that arbour, while that she
    With melting kisses
    Distilling blisses
From her free lips, for joy did ravish me,
The pretty nightingale did sing melodiously.

Hail to those groves, where we enjoyed our loves
    So many days!
May trees there be springing and the pretty birds be
        singing
    Their roundelays.
Oh! may the grass grow ever green
    On which we lying
    Have oft been trying
More several ways of pleasure than that queen,
Which once in bed with Mars by all the gods was seen.

ANON

Down in a Garden

DOWN in a garden sat my dearest Love,
Her skin more soft and white than down of swan,
More tender-hearted than the turtle-dove,
And far more kind than bleeding pelican.
I courted her; she rose and blushing said,
'Why was I born to live and die a maid?'
With that I plucked a pretty marigold,
Whose dewy leaves shut up when day is done:
'Sweeting,' I said, 'arise, look and behold,
A pretty riddle I'll to thee unfold:
These leaves shut in as close as cloistered nun,
Yet will they open when they see the sun.'
'What mean you by this riddle, sir?' she said,
'I pray expound it.' Then I thus began:
'Know maids are made for men, man for a maid.'
With that she changed her colour and grew wan:
'Since that this riddle you so well unfold,
Be you the sun, I'll be the marigold.'

ANON

By A Bank Of Pinks And Lilies

Do not ask me, charming Phillis,
   Why I lead you here alone,
By this bank of pinks and lilies
   And of roses newly blown.

'Tis not to behold the beauty
   Of those flowers that crown the spring;
'Tis to—but I know my duty,
   And dare never name the thing.

('Tis, at worst, but her denying;
Why should I thus fearful be?
Every minute, gently flying,
   Smiles and says, 'Make use of me.')

What the sun does to those roses,
  While the beams play sweetly in,
I would—but my fear opposes,
  And I dare not name the thing.

Yet I die, if I conceal it;
  Ask my eyes, or ask your own;
And if neither can reveal it,
  Think what lovers think alone.

On this bank of pinks and lilies,
  Might I speak what I would do;
I would with my lovely Phillis—
  I would; I would—Ah! would *you*?

ANON

I Have a Garden

I have a garden of my own,
But so with roses overgrown
And lilies that you would it guess
To be a little wilderness:
And all the spring-time of the year
It only lovèd to be there.
Among the beds of lilies I
Have sought it oft where it should lie;
Yet could not, till itself would rise,
Find it although before mine eyes:
For in the flaxen lilies' shade
It like a bank of lilies laid.
Upon the roses it would feed,
Until its lips e'en seem'd to bleed:
And then to me 'twould boldly trip,
And print those roses on my lip.
But all its chief delight was still
On roses thus itself to fill,
And its pure virgin limbs to fold
In whitest sheets of lilies cold:
Had it lived long it would have been
Lilies without—roses within.

ANDREW MARVELL

In Paradise

AND now what monarch would not gardener be,
My fair Amanda's stately gait to see?
How her feet tempt! how soft and light she treads,
Fearing to wake the flowers from their beds!
Yet from their sweet green pillows everywhere,
They start and gaze about to see my Fair.
Look at yon flower yonder, how it grows
Sensibly! how it opes its leaves and blows,
Puts its best Easter clothes on, neat and gay:
Amanda's presence makes it holiday!
Look how on tiptoe that fair lily stands
To look on thee, and court thy whiter hands
To gather it! I saw in yonder crowd—
That tulip bed of which Dame Flora's proud—
A short dwarf flower did enlarge its stalk,
And shoot an inch to see Amanda walk.
Nay, look, my Fairest! look how fast they grow
Into a scaffold-method spring, as though,
Riding to Parliament, were to be seen
In pomp and state some royal amorous Queen!
The gravelled walks, though even as a die,
Lest some loose pebble should offensive lie,
Quilt themselves o'er with downy moss for thee;
The walls are hanged with blossomed tapestry
To hide their nakedness when looked upon;
The maiden fig tree puts Eve's apron on;
The broad-leaved sycamore, and every tree,
Shakes like the trembling asp, and bends to thee,
And each leaf proudly strives, with fresher air
To fan the curlëd tresses of thy hair.
Nay, and the bee too, with his wealthy thigh,
Mistakes his hive, and to thy lips doth fly,
Willing to treasure up his honey there,
Where honey-combs so sweet and plenty are.
Look how that pretty modest columbine
Hangs down its head, to view those feet of thine!
See the fond motion of the strawberry,
Creeping on th' earth, to go along with thee!
The lovely violet makes after too,
Unwilling yet, my dear, to part with you;
The knot-grass and the daisies catch thy toes,

To kiss my fair one's feet before she goes;
All court and wish me lay Amanda down,
And give my dear a new green-flowered gown.
  Come, let me kiss thee falling, kiss at rise,
  Thou in the garden, I in Paradise.

NATHANIEL HOOKES

An Invitation

O Lady, leave thy silken thread
  And flowery tapestrie,
There's living roses on the bush,
  And blossoms on the tree;
Stoop where thou wilt, thy careless hand
  Some random bud will meet;
Thou canst not tread, but thou wilt find
  The daisy at thy feet.

'Tis like the birthday of the world,
  When earth was born in bloom;
The light is made of many dyes,
  The air is all perfume;
There's crimson buds, and white and blue—
  The very rainbow showers
Have turned to blossoms where they fell,
  And sown the earth with flowers.

There's fairy tulips in the East,
  The garden of the sun;
The very streams reflect the hues,
  And blossom as they run:
While morn opes like a crimson rose,
  Still wet with pearly showers;
Then, Lady, leave the silken thread
  Thou twinest into flowers.

THOMAS HOOD

Now Sleeps the Crimson Petal

Now sleeps the crimson petal, now the white;
Nor waves the cypress in the palace walk;
Nor winks the gold fin in the porphyry font:
The fire-fly wakens: waken thou with me.

Now droops the milkwhite peacock like a ghost,
And like a ghost she glimmers on to me.

Now lies the Earth all Danaë to the stars,
And all thy heart lies open unto me.

Now slides the silent meteor on, and leaves
A shining furrow, as thy thoughts in me.

Now folds the lily all her sweetness up,
And slips into the bosom of the lake:
So fold thyself, my dearest, thou, and slip
Into my bosom and be lost in me.

ALFRED, LORD TENNYSON

The Flower's Name

Here's the garden she walked across,
    Arm in my arm, such a short while since:
Hark, now I push its wicket, the moss
    Hinders the hinges and makes them wince!
She must have reached this shrub ere she turned,
    As back with that murmur the wicket swung;
For she laid the poor snail, my chance foot spurned,
    To feed and forget it the leaves among.

Down this side of the gravel-walk
    She went while her robe's edge brushed the box:
And here she paused in her gracious talk
    To point me a moth on the milk-white phlox.
Roses, ranged in valiant row,
    I will never think that she passed you by!

She loves you noble roses, I know;
   But yonder, see, where the rock-plants lie!

This flower she stopped at, finger on lip,
   Stooped over, in doubt, as settling its claim;
Till she gave me, with pride to make no slip,
   Its soft meandering Spanish name:
What a name! Was it love, or praise?
   Speech half-asleep, or song half-awake?
I must learn Spanish, one of these days,
   Only for that slow sweet name's sake.

Roses, if I live and do well,
   I may bring her, one of these days,
To fix you fast with as fine a spell,
   Fit you each with his Spanish phrase;
But do not detain me now; for she lingers
   There, like sunshine over the ground,
And ever I see her soft white fingers
   Searching after the bud she found.

Flower, you Spaniard, look that you grow not,
   Stay as you are and be loved for ever!
Bud, if I kiss you 'tis that you blow not,
   Mind, the shut pink mouth opens never!
For while thus it pouts, her fingers wrestle,
   Twinkling the audacious leaves between,
Till found they turn and down they nestle—
   Is not the dear mark still to be seen?

Where I find her not, beauties vanish;
   Whither I follow her, beauties flee;
Is there no method to tell her in Spanish
   June's twice June since she breathed it with me?
Come, bud, show me the least of her traces,
   Treasure my lady's lightest footfall
—Ah, you may flout and turn up your faces—
   Roses, you are not so fair after all!

ROBERT BROWNING

First Love

I have been in this garden of unripe fruit
All the long day,
Where cold and clear from the hard green apples
The light fell away.

I was wand'ring here with my own true love
But as I bent o'er
She dwindled back to her childhood again
And I saw her no more.

A wind sprang up and a hail of buds
About me rolled,
Then this fog I knew before I was born
Except for the cold.

                              HUGH MacDIARMID

To a Prodigal Old Maid

Sing now no hymn nor chant a dirge
Nor weep for any dead thing,
Still in her veins an ardent sting
Her beating blood can urge

To the white pale lily she is kind,
Rearing few flowers that are red,
Yet sometimes weeds grow there instead...
In the conservatory of her mind.

A quick caress she gives the rose,
Lilac, geranium–all in season...
Oh, if she might have seen a reason
For powdering her nose!

Too deft at lavender and chintz,
Too cold for wooing but not wan,
She dreams a springtime gentleman
To have come a springtime since.

                              ALLEN TATE

The Happy Watering-Pot

'I have forgotten my flowers,' said the spinster aunt.

'Water them now,' said Mr Tupman, in accents of persuasion.

'You will take cold in the evening air,' urged the spinster aunt, affectionately.

'No, no,' said Mr Tupman, rising; 'it will do me good. Let me accompany you.'

The lady paused to adjust the sling in which the left arm of the youth was placed, and taking his right arm led him to the garden.

There was a bower at the further end, with honey-suckle, jessamine, and creeping plants—one of those sweet retreats, which humane men erect for the accommodation of spiders.

The spinster aunt took up a large watering-pot which lay in one corner, and was about to leave the arbour. Mr Tupman detained her, and drew her to a seat beside him.

'Miss Wardle!' said he.

The spinster aunt trembled, till some pebbles which had accidentally found their way into the large watering-pot, shook like an infant's rattle.

'Miss Wardle,' said Mr Tupman, 'you are an angel.'

'Mr Tupman!' exclaimed Rachel, blushing as red as the watering-pot itself.

'Nay,' said the eloquent Pickwickian— 'I know it but too well.'

'All women are angels, they say,' murmured the lady, playfully.

'Then what can *you* be; or to what, without presumption, can I compare you?' replied Mr Tupman. 'Where was the woman ever seen, who resembled you? Where else could I hope to find so rare a combination of excellence and beauty? Where else could I seek to—— Oh!' Here Mr Tupman paused, and pressed the hand which clasped the handle of the happy watering-pot.

CHARLES DICKENS

Picking Apples

Apple time, and the trees brittle with fruit.
My children climb the bent, half-sapping branches
to where the apples, cheeked with the hectic flush
of Autumn, hang. The children bark their haunches

and lean on the edge of their balance. The apples are out
of reach; so they shake the tree. Through a tussle of leaves and
     laughter
the apples thud down; thud on the orchard grasses
in rounded, grave finality, each one after

the other dropping; the muffled sound of them dropping
like suddenly hearing the beats of one's own heart
falling away, as if shaken by some storm
as localised as this. Loading them into the cart,

the sweet smell of their bruises moist in the sun,
their skin's bloom tacky against the touch,
I experience fulfilment, suddenly aware
of some ripe, wordless answer, knowing no such

answers exist; only questions, questions, the beating years,
the dropped apples... the kind of touch and go
that poetry makes satisfaction of;
reality, with nothing more to show

than a brush of branches, time and the apples falling,
and shrill among the leaves, children impatiently calling.

                                        MAURICE LINDSAY

In The North

Light fades slowly in the long evenings of May and June
here in the north. The eyes adjust
and when I straighten up from a seedbed
I can still make out the darker shapes of the swifts
against an archipelago of clouds
and the outline of a thrush
singing from the top branch of a plum tree.

I feel the stiffness and the aching satisfaction of tasks.
I put the tools away
while I can still see the path to the outhouse.
Indoors, I switch on the light
and begin to wash off the stains of earth and calomel dust.

The thrush calls out and I look from the window
on to an incomprehensible darkness.

I stare until I see the deeper mass
of apple trees and plum trees
and the boundary wall,
black shapes with nothing in between them
except the glint of glass in the greenhouse
and my reflection out there
waiting like another self at ease in the night.

                                        JAMES AITCHISON

PRACTICALITIES

Zeal Continuously

The gardener must not be slothful but full of zeal continuously. Nor must he despise hardening his hands with toil...I plant my seeds and the kindly dew moistens them. Should drought prevail, I must water it, letting the drops fall through my fingers, for the impetus of a full stream from a water-pot would disturb my seedlings. Part of my garden is hard and dry under the shadow of a roof; in another part a high brick wall robs it of sun and air. Even here something will at last succeed!

WALAFRED STRABO

Garden Produce

As to the produce of a Garden, every middle-aged person of observation may perceive, within his own memory, both in town and country, how vastly the consumption of vegetables is increased. Green stalls in cities now support multitudes in a comfortable state, while gardeners get fortunes. Every decent labourer also has his garden, which is half his support as well as his delight; and common farmers provide plenty of beans, peas, and greens, for their hands to eat with their bacon; and those few that do not are despised for their sordid parsimony, and looked upon as regardless of the welfare of their dependants. Potatoes have prevailed in this little district by means of premiums, within these twenty years only, and are much esteemed here now by the poor, who would scarce have ventured to taste them in the last reign.

Our Saxon ancestors certainly had some sort of cabbage, because they call the month of February Sprout-cale; but long after their days, the cultivation of gardens was little attended to. The religious being men of leisure, and keeping up a constant correspondence with Italy, were the first people among us that had gardens and fruit-trees in any perfection, within the walls of their abbies, priories, and monasteries, where the lamp of knowledge continued to burn, however dimly. In them men of business were formed for the state: the art of writing was cultivated by the monks; they were the only proficients in mechanics, gardening, and architecture. The

barons neglected every pursuit that did not lead to war, or tend to
the pleasure of the chase.

GILBERT WHITE OF SELBORNE

A Kitchen Garden

Lavender, sweet-briar, orris. Here
Shall Beauty make her pomander,
Her sweet-balls for to lay in clothes
That wrap her as the leaves the rose.

Take roses red and lilies white,
A kitchen garden's my delight;
Its gillyflowers and phlox and cloves,
And its tall cote of irised doves.

KATHERINE TYNAN

The Kitchen Garden

Every kitchen-garden ought, if possible, to be either square or
oblong, for the convenience of planting the beds, and you will find
a garden of one acre in extent quite as much as you will be able to
manage. I would advise you to have it surrounded by a wall about
ten feet high for fruit trees; and in front of this wall there should be
a border ten or twelve feet wide; beyond which should be a gravel
walk four feet wide, leaving a square or oblong plot of ground in
the centre for culinary vegetables. This central plot may either have
a main walk up the centre, and two or three side walks, or be left
all in one bed, which may be divided into compartments, with paths
between, to suit the convenience of the gardener. The best situation
for your kitchen-garden will be as near the stable as possible for
the convenience of manure; and, of course, it will join the reserve
ground. The surface of the ground should be level, or gently sloping
to the south, and there should be no high trees near it. The whole of
the garden should be well drained, and you should contrive it so as
to have easy access to either pond or river water. A valley or a hill
is a bad situation for a kitchen-garden; as the valley is very liable to
injury from frost, on account of the damps that hang over it; and the

hill is not only cold, but exposed to injury from high winds.

I have already mentioned that the form of a kitchen-garden should be either square or oblong; and I may add, that the walks should always be straight, as, if they were serpentine, it would be difficult to wheel a barrow of manure along them without overturning it. The square form of the garden, however, is not only on account of the walks, but in order that the compartment in the centre may be divided into oblong beds, as it is most convenient to sow vegetables in straight lines to allow of weeding and hoeing between them, earthing them up, &c.

JANE LOUDON

Digging

Digging is the first operation neccessary in gardening, as nothing can be done in the way of cultivating the soil till it has been first pulverised, so as to allow the fine delicate roots of the plants to penetrate among its particles. It is also necessary that the air should have access to the roots of plants, as they depend for their nourishment almost as much on the carbon and other elements which they absorb from the air, as on those which they obtain from the soil. On this account it is necessary, not only to dig the soil well before anything is planted in it, but also to fork it over occasionally whenever its surface becomes hardened and impervious to the air and rain. When manure is applied also, it is customary to dig it into the soil; and ground is occasionally trenched in order to bring up fresh soil to the surface, whenever the surface soil appears to be exhausted and to want renewing. The operation of digging requires considerable strength, as it requires first to be able to force the spade into the ground, and then to raise as much earth as will lie upon the spade and turn it over. It is, however, a fine healthy occupation, not only from its calling the muscles into vigorous action, but from the smell of the new earth being particularly invigorating; and you might have a lady's spade, with a smooth willow handle, that will enable you to dig a small bed without much difficulty. You will be surprised, however, to find, if you try the experiment, that there is an art in digging as well as in everything else; and that it is extremely difficult, both to dig in a straight line, and to make the ground look even tolerably level after it has been dug over.

JANE LOUDON

A Spade

Cicely:	When I see a spade I call it a spade.
Gwendolen:	I am glad to say I have never seen a spade. It is obvious that our social spheres have been widely different.

OSCAR WILDE

Planting

Planting is one of my great amusements, and even of those things which can only be for posterity, for a Septuagenery has no right to count on anything beyond annuals.

THOMAS JEFFERSON

How To Lay Grass

To lay grass, first level the ground, whether a walke or a plot; and 'tis the better to lye a year so made up, before you lay the turf; because it may be levelled up again, if it sink into holes; if it lye wet, bottom with stones and rubbish; and if the earth be fat, take it out, and put in sand...Let the turf be of equal thickness, near inch and a half thick, a foot and a half broad, and as much in length; lay their green sides together when you put them in the cart, but do not roll them when brought home. Lay them all even and close, feeling each particular turf with your foot, so as you may discern any inequality, to be helped immediately.

JOHN REID

Pruning

Begin betimes to prune your fruit-trees; spare them not while young; reduce them into good shape and order while such, so they will not only overgrow their wounds, their branches being but small, but also, when they should come to bear fruit, you shall not need to

cut so much, only purge them of superfluities; and this is the way
to make trees fruitful as well as pleasant.

JOHN REID

Weed Puller

Under the concrete benches,
Hacking at black hairy roots,—
Those lewd monkey-tails hanging from drainholes,—
Digging into the soft rubble underneath,
Webs and weeds,
Grubs and snails and sharp sticks,
Or yanking tough fern-shapes,
Coiled green and thick, like dripping smilax,
Tugging all day at perverse life:
The indignity of it!—
With everything blooming above me,
Lilies, pale-pink cyclamen, roses,
Whole fields lovely and inviolate,—
Me down in that fetor of weeds,
Crawling on all fours,
Alive, in a slippery grave.

THEODORE ROETHKE

The Merits of Mould

There are, I confess, who fancy that this long exposure of earth,
before it be employed for a crop, causes it to exhale, and spend the
virtue which it should retain; but, provided nothing be suffered to
grow on it, whilst it lies thus rough and fallow, there is no danger
of that, there being in truth no compost or laetation whatsoever
comparable to this continual motion, repastination, and turning of
the Mould with a spade, the pared-off turf (which is the very fat and
efflorescence of the earth) and even weeds with their vegetable salts,
collected into heaps and exposed, when reduced, fall into natural,
sweet, and excellent Mould. I say, this is a marvellous advantage,
and does in greater measure fertilize the ground alone, without any

other addition; for the earth, which was formerly dull and unactive, or perhaps producing but one kind of plant, will by this culture dispose itself to bring forth variety, as it lies in depths, be it never so profound, cold and crude, the nature of the plant always following the genius of the soil; but indeed requiring time, according to the depth from whence you fetch it, to purge and prepare itself, and render it fit for conception, evaporating the malignant halituses and impurities of the imprisoned air, laxing the parts, and giving easy deliverance to its offspring.

JOHN EVELYN

A Stercorarious Heap

The stable yields a stercorarious heap,
Impregnated with quick fermenting salts,
And potent to resist the freezing blast:
For ere the beech and elm have cast their leaf
Deciduous, and when now November dark
Checks vegetation in the torpid plant
Exposed to his cold breath, the task begins.
                    That where he builds
Th'agglomerated pile, his frame may front
The sun's meridian dusk, and at the back
Enjoy close shelter, wall, or reeds, or hedge
Impervious to the wind. First he bids spread
Dry fern or litter'd hay, that may imbibe
Th' ascending damps; then leisurely impose,
And lightly, shaking it with agile hand
From the full fork, the saturated straw.
What longest binds the closest, forms secure
The shapely side, that as it rises takes
By just degrees an overhanging breadth,
Shelt'ring the base with its projected eaves.
Th'uplifted frame compact at ev'ry joint,
And overlaid with clear translucent glass
He settles next upon the sloping mount,
Whose sharp declivity shoots off secure
From the dash'd pane the deluge as it falls.
He shuts it close, and the first labor ends.

WILLIAM COWPER

Lime Rubbish

Lime rubbish dug in among the roots of ivy encourages it much.

SIR WALTER SCOTT

A Use for a Potato

The cutting of an apple-tree, or other fruit-tree, may be preserved by sticking it into a potato and planting both together.

SIR WALTER SCOTT

Privacy

Love your neighbour, yet pull not down your hedge.

GEORGE HERBERT

Tools

Few lend (but fools)
Their working Tools

THOMAS TUSSER

The Art of Laying Out Gardens

The art of laying out gardens consists in an endeavour to combine cheerfulness of aspect, luxuriance of growth, shade, solitude and repose, in such a manner that the senses may be deluded by an imitation of rural nature. Diversity, which is the main advantage of free landscape, must, therefore, be sought in a judicious choice of soil, an alteration of chains of hills and valleys, gorge, brooks and lakes covered with aquatic plants. Symmetry is wearying, and ennui and disgust will soon be excited in a garden where every part betrays constraint and art.

LIEN-TSCHEN

Effects

The bright acacia, and the vivid plane,
The rich laburnum with its golden chain;
And all the variegated flow'ring race,
That deck the garden, and the shrubb'ry grace,
Should near to buildings, or to water grow,
Where bright reflections beam with equal glow,
And blending vivid tints with vivid light,
The whole in brilliant harmony unite:
E'en the bright flow'rets' tints will dim appear,
When limpid waters foam and glitter near,
And o'er their curling crystals sparkling play
The clear reflection of meridian day;
From buildings, too, strong refluent lights are thrown,
When the sun downward shines upon the stone;
Or on the windows darts its evening rays,
And makes the glass with fire responsive blaze.

RICHARD PAYNE KNIGHT

Of Gardens

Nor with too hasty Care presume to sow,
E'er yet the Nature of the Soil you know,
A Soil where Moisture rules your Flow'rs demand,
Endow their Beauties with the richest Land:
Shun lean white Clay where painted Lizards lye,
Or Stony Ground, or Earth with Chalk to dry:
And test the Turf e'en with a ruddy Soil,
With barren clods should mock the Gard'ner's Toil,
Search deep the Mould, nor the green Turf believe,
Oft with the surface of a Soil deceive.
Rough Gravel may a verdant Coat display,
And Grass may live upon a burning Clay;
The Coarcer Moulds experinc'd Artists sift,
Through wire-wrought Sieves till not a Pebble's left;
Which rudely might the tender Blossoms wound,
Or notch th' imprison'd Blade in Fetters bound.

When both your Heav'n and Earth are close with
   Care,
(A kindly Soil depends on kindly Air.)

       *   *   *   *   *

Two rules in sowing with your Art unfold,
What face of Heav'n to choose, what depths of mould.

LE PÈRE RENÉ RAPIN

A Gardening Rule

I have been asked by some, who seem to think that I grow many
plants which are not usually seen in gardens of hardy plants, to
say if I have any special rules for the successful cultivation of them.
I know of no secrets in gardening, and I do not work or manage the
garden on any hard-and-fast rules. If I have any rule, it is to leave
my plants as much as possible to nature, and to let them grow in the
ways which they choose for themselves. For this reason I dislike all
tyings and nailings, all sticks, and everything that tends to cramp the
free growth of the plants. Of course there is a limit to this freedom
of growth; some plants must be tied for their own protection against
wind, but such tying should be done as early as possible, for it is with
plants as with ourselves, that the right way to train them in the way
they should go is to commence with the 'child'. But for most plants
I prefer cages. They are made, of different heights and diameters,
of iron (technically called 'three-quarter round'), with three or four
uprights and a few hoops. They are cheaply made, and last for ever;
and I leave them in the ground all the winter, so that when the plants
sprout in the spring they at once adapt themselves to the cage that
surrounds them, and soon hide it with their foliage. It may seem
a paradox to talk of a free natural growth and yet to recommend a
constant use of the pruning-knife, but in practice the one is necessary
to the other; and in nothing is the gardener's skill more shown than
in the judicious use of the pruning-knife.

CANON HENRY ELLACOMBE

Putrifactions and Excrements

Some putrifactions and excrements do yield excellent odours: as civis and musk, and, as some think, ambergris... The senses love not to be over-pleased, but to have a commixture of somewhat that is in itself ingrate. Certainly we see how discords in music, falling upon concords, make the sweetest strains; and we see again what strange tastes delight the taste, as red herrings, caviare, parmesan, &c. And it may be the same holdeth in smells.

FRANCIS BACON

The Beautiful Lawn Sprinkler

What gives it power makes it change its mind
At each extreme, and lean its rising rain
Down low, first one and then the other way;
In which exchange humility and pride
Reverse, forgive, arise, and then die again,
Wherefore it holds at both ends of the day
The rainbow in its scattering grains of spray.

HAROLD NEMEROV

A Fountain

There is a fountain rising in the upper part of my garden, which forms a little wandering rill, and administers to the pleasure as well as the plenty of the place. I have so conducted it that it visits most of my plantations; and have taken particular care to let it run in the same manner as it would do in an open field, so that it generally passes through banks of violets and primroses, plats of willow or other plants, that seem to be of its own producing.

JOSEPH ADDISON

Fountains

Fountains...are a Great Beauty and Refreshment, but Pools mar all, and make the Garden unwholesome, and full of Flies and Frogs. Fountains I intend to be one of two Natures: the one that sprinkleth or spouteth Water, the other a fair Receipt of Water, of some thirty or forty foot square, but without Fish, or Slime, or Mud. For the first, the Ornaments of Images Gilt, or of Marble, which are in use, do well; but the main matter is, so to convey the Water, as it never stay, either in the Bowls, or in the Cistern, that the Water be never by rest discoloured, Green, or Red, or the like; or gather any Mossiness or Putrefaction. Besides that, it is to be cleansed every day by the hand; also some steps up to it, and some Fine Pavement about it, doth well. As for the other kind of Fountain, which we may call a Bathing Pool, it may admit much Curiosity and Beauty, wherewith we will not trouble ourselves, as, that the Bottom be finely paved, and with Images, the Sides likewise; and withal Embellished with coloured Glass, and such things of Lustre; Encompassed also with fine Rails of low Statua's. But the main point is the same, which we mentioned in the former kind of Fountain, which is, that the Water be in perpetual Motion, fed by a Water higher than the Pool, and delivered into it by fair Spouts, and then discharged away under Ground by some Equality of Bores, that it stay little. And for fine Devices, of Arching water without spilling, and making it rise in Several forms (of Feathers, Drinking Glasses, Canopies, and the like) they be pretty things to look on, but nothing to Health and Sweetness.

FRANCIS BACON

Sundial Mottoes

HORE. PARS. VITAE
(Every Hour shortens life)

FUGIO. FUGE.
(I stay for no man)

NON. SEMPER. ERUNT. SATURNALIA.
(Take time by the Forelock)

YOU. MAY. HASTE. BUT. CANNOT. STOP. ME.
(On an old church at Tunbridge Wells)

TRIFLE. NOT. YOUR. TIME'S SHORT.

IT. IS. LATER. THAN. YOU. THINK.

NOW. IS. YESTERDAY'S. TOMORROW.

TAK. TINT. O. TIME. ERE. TIME. TAK. TINT. O. THEE.

'TIS. ALWAYS. MORNING. SOMEWHERE. IN. THE. WORLD.

> Supreme he stands among the flowers
> And only marks Life's sunny hours.
> For him dull days do not exist—
> The brazen-faced old optimist.

For a Sundial

> Hold not the hour,
> Loving what you have lost;
> Only the gifted hour can be your guest:
> Gladly accept the flower and the frost:
> The sun goes down and shadows are at rest.

WILLIAM SOUTAR

The Greenhouse

Who loves a garden, loves a greenhouse too.
Unconscious of a less propitious clime
There blooms exotic beauty, warm and snug,
While the winds whistle and the snows descend.
The spiry myrtle with unwith'ring leaf
Shines there and flourishes. The golden boast
Of Portugal and Western India there,
The ruddier orange and the paler lime,

Peep through their polish'd foliage at the storm,
And seem to smile at what they need not fear.

Th' amomum there with intermingling flow'rs
And cherries hangs her twigs. Geranium boasts
Her crimson honours, and the spangled beau,
Ficoides, glitters bright the winter long.
All plants, of ev'ry leaf, that can endure
The winter's frown if screen'd from his shrewd bite,
Live there and prosper. Those Ausonia claims,
Levantine regions these; th' Azores send
Their jessamine; her jessamine remote
Caffraria: foreigners from many lands,
They form one social shade, as if convened
By magic summons of th' Orphean lyre.
Yet just arrangement, rarely brought to pass
But by a master's hand, disposing well
The gay diversities of leaf and flow'r,
Must lend its aid t'illustrate all their charms,
And dress the regular yet various scene.

                        Much yet remains
Unsung, and many cares are yet behind
And more laborious. Cares on which depends
Their vigour, injured soon, not soon restored.
The soil must be renew'd, which often wash'd
Loses its treasure of salubrious salts,
And disappoints the roots; the slender roots,
Close interwoven where they meet the vase,
Must smooth be shorn away; the sapless branch
Must fly before the knife; the wither'd leaf
Must be detach'd, and where it strews the floor
Swept with a women's neatness, breeding else
Contagion, and disseminating death.
Discharge but these kind offices, (and who
Would spare, that loves them, offices like these?)
Well they reward the toil. The sight is pleased,
The scent regaled, each odorif'rous leaf,
Each op'ning blossom freely breathes abroad
Its gratitude, and thanks him with its sweets.

                              WILLIAM COWPER

Peace in the Greenhouse

To go to the greenhouse when the weather is wild, to close the door, to stand and listen to the wind outside, to the rain that slashes the frail roof, to see, through the misted glass, the black, storm-tossed branches of distant elms, to take a deep breath, to savour to the full the strange and almost uncanny peace which this frail tenement creates... to me this is one of the truest joys which life has given.

There is a sense of escape...a sense of sanctuary. Thus, perhaps, felt the fugitives, as they clutched the altar rails when the mob was fierce behind them. For here no harm can come. No bitter wind can assault, no frost can chill. I pray, indeed, that the storm outside may increase, that the wind may rise more strongly, that the rain may turn to sleet, and beat a devilish but impotent tattoo on the crystal roof. All the sweeter, then, is the strange security of the greenhouse.

BEVERLEY NICHOLS

Magic

I love a still conservatory
    That's full of giant, breathless palms,
Azaleas, clematis and vines,
    Whose quietness great Trees becalms
Filling the air with foliage,
    A curved and dreamy statuary.

I love to hear a cold, pure rill
    Of water trickling low, afar
With sudden little jerks and purls
    Into a tank or stoneware jar,
The song of a tiny sleeping bird
    Held like a shadow in its trill.

I love the mossy quietness
   That grows upon the great stone flags,
The dark tree-ferns, the staghorn ferns,
   The prehistoric, antlered stags
That carven stand and stare among
   The silent, ferny wilderness.

And are they birds or souls that flit
   Among the trees so silently,
And are they fish or ghosts that haunt
   The still pools of the rockery!
For I am but a sculptured rock
   As in that magic place I sit...

I watch a white Nyanza float
   Upon a green, untroubled pool,
A fairyland Ophelia, she
   Has cast herself in water cool,
And lies while fairy cymbals ring
   Drowned in her fairy castle moat.

The goldfish sing a winding song
   Below her pale and waxen face,
The water-nymph is dancing by
   Lifting smooth arms with mournful grace,
A stainless white dream she floats on
   While fairies beat a fairy gong.

Silent the Cattleyas blaze
   And thin red orchid shapes of Death
Peer savagely with twisted lips
   Sucking an eerie, phantom breath
With that bright, spotted, fever'd lust
   That watches lonely travellers craze.

Gigantic, mauve and hairy leaves
   Hang like obliterated faces
Full of dim unattained expression
   Such as haunts virgin forest places
When Silence leaps among the trees
   And the echoing heart deceives.

                W J TURNER

Garden Centre

Gardeners speculate, wandering dwarf-hedged paths;
sunlight winks their cars, as if in the know
how hard it is to persuade bought seeds to grow
the flourish on the packet. Plastic baths,
moulded for sunken pools, lie stacked like plates;
labels on roses flutter at hardy shrubs,
leading to fertilisers, sprays for grubs
and, beyond, the furniture, fences, seats and gates.
Commotioning their corner, a painted knot
of gnomes drop fishing lines that never go taut,
smirking with tweesome glee, as if each had caught
whatever answered the need a customer sought.
What they'd pulled up's a different kettle of fish,
tangled with make-believing and rootless wish.

                                        MAURICE LINDSAY

The Seed Shop

Here in a quiet and dusty room they lie,
    Faded as crumbled stone or shifting sand,
Forlorn as ashes, shrivelled, scentless, dry,
    Meadows and gardens running through my hand.

Dead that shall quicken at the trump of Spring,
    Sleepers to stir beneath June's splendid kiss,
Though birds pass over, unremembering,
    And no bee seek here roses that were his.

In this brown husk a dale of hawthorn dreams,
    A cedar in this narrow cell is thrust
That will drink deeply of a century's streams;
    These lilies shall make Summer on my dust.

Here in their safe and simple house of death,
    Sealed in their shells a million roses leap;
Here I can blow a garden with my breath,
    And in my hand a forest lies asleep.

                                        MURIEL STUART

A Cabinet of Seeds Displayed

These are the original monies of the earth,
In which invested, as the spark in fire,
They will produce a green wealth toppling tall,
A trick they do by dying, by decay,
In burial becoming each his kind
To rise in glory and be magnified
A million times above the obscure grave.

Reader, these samples are exhibited
For contemplation, locked in potency
And kept from act for reverence's sake.
May they remind us while we live on earth
That all economies are primitive;
And by their reservations may they teach
Our governors, who speak of husbandry
And think the hurricane, where power lies.

HOWARD NEMEROV

Topiary

How contrary to this simplicity (of Homer) is the modern practice of
gardening! We seem to make it our study to recede from nature, not
only in the various tonsure of greens into the most regular and formal
shape, but even in monstrous attempts beyond the reach of the art
itself: we run into sculpture, and are the better pleased to have our
trees in the most awkward figures of men and animals, than in the
most regular of their own...

A citizen is no sooner proprietor of a couple of yews, but he
entertains thoughts of erecting them into giants, like those of
Guildhall. I know an eminent cook, who beautified his country
seat with a coronation dinner in greens, where you see the champion
flourishing on horseback at one end of the table, and the Queen in
perpetual youth at the other.

For the benefit of all my loving countrymen of this curious taste,
I shall here publish a catalogue of greens to be disposed of by an

eminent town gardener, who has lately applied to me upon this head...

I proceed to this catalogue.

Adam and Eve in yew; Adam a little shattered by the fall of the tree of knowledge in the great storm:
Eve and the serpent very flourishing.
The tower of Babel not yet finished.
St George in box; his arm scarce long enough, but will be in condition to stick the dragon by next April.
A green dragon of the same, with a tail of ground ivy for the present.
N B These two not to be sold separately.
Edward the Black Prince in cypress.
A laurestine bear in blossom, with a juniper hunter in berries.
A pair of giants, stunted, to be sold cheap.
A queen Elizabeth in phylyraea, a little inclining to the green sickness, but of full growth.
An old maid of honour in wormwood.
A topping Ben Jonson in laurel
Diverse eminent modern poets in bays, somewhat blighted, to be disposed of, a pennyworth.
A quickset hog, shot up into a procupine, by its being forgot a week in rainy weather.
A lavender pig, with sage growing in his belly.
Noah's ark in holly, standing on the mount; the ribs a little damaged for want of water.

ALEXANDER POPE

Suburban Life

Suburban villas, highway-side retreats,
That dread th' encroachment of our growing streets,
Tight boxes, neatly sash'd, and in a blaze
With all a July sun's collected rays,
Delight the citizen, who, gasping there,
Breathes clouds of dust, and calls it country air.
Oh sweet retirement, who would balk the thought,
That could afford retirement, or could not?
'Tis such an easy walk, so smooth and straight,
The second milestone fronts the garden gate;
A step if fair, and, if a shower approach,
You find safe shelter in the next stage-coach.
There, prison'd in a parlour snug and small,
Like bottled wasps upon a southern wall,
The man of business and his friends compress'd,
Forget their labours, and yet find no rest;
But still 'tis rural—trees are to be seen
From ev'ry window, and the fields are green;
Ducks paddle in the pond before the door,
And what could a remoter scene show more?

WILLIAM COWPER

Dirty and Amused

And so you have a garden of your own, and you plant and trans-
plant, and are dirty and amused; are you not ashamed of yourself?
Why, I have no such thing, you monster; nor ever shall be either dirty
or amused as long as I live! My gardens are in a window like those of
a lodger up three pairs of stairs in Petticoat Lane or Camomile Street,
and they go to bed regularly under the same roof that I do.

THOMAS GRAY

THE MONTHS

A Child's Calendar

No visitors in January.
A snowman smokes a cold pipe in the yard.

They stand about like ancient women,
The February hills.
They have seen many a coming and going, the hills.

In March, Moorfea is littered
With knock-kneed lambs.

Daffodils at the door in April,
Three shawled Marys.
A lark splurges in galilees of sky.

And in May
A russet stallion shoulders the hill apart.
The mares tremble.

The June bee
Bumps in the pane with a heavy bag of plunder.

Strangers swarm in July
With cameras, binoculars, bird books.

He thumped the crag in August,
A blind blue whale.

September crofts get wrecked in blond surges.
They struggle, the harvesters.
They drag loaf and ale-kirn into winter.

In October the fishmonger
Argues, pleads, threatens at the shore.

Nothing in November
But tinkers at the door, keening, with cans.

Some December midnight
Christ, lord, lie warm in our byre.
Here are stars, an ox, poverty enough.

GEORGE MACKAY BROWN

January by this Fire...

Januar	By thys fyre I warme my handys;
Februar	And with my spade I delfe my landys.
Marche	Here I sette my thynge to sprynge;
Aprille	And here I here the fowlis synge.
Maij	I am as lyght as byrde in bowe;
Junij	And I wede my corne well I-now.
Julij	With my sythe my mede I mawe;
Auguste	And here I shere my corne full lowe.
September	With my flayll I erne my brede;
October	And here I sawe my whete so rede.
November	At Martynesmasse I kylle my swyne;
December	And at Christesmasse I drynke redde wyne.

ANON

The Year

The crocus while the days are dark,
    Unfolds its saffron sheen;
At April's touch, the crudest bark
    Discovers gems of green.

Then sleep the seasons, full of might;
    While slowly swells the pod
And rounds the peach, and in the night
    The mushroom bursts the sod.

The winter comes: the frozen rut
    Is bound with silver bars;
The snowdrift heaps against the hut;
    And night is pierced with stars.

COVENTRY PATMORE

Janiveer

The blackest month of all the year
Is the month of Janiveer.

OLD SAYING

February Tasks

In February the farmer shall make ready his garden grounds to sow
and set therein al manner of herbs. He shall repair the hedges of
his garden. He shall buy Bees, he shall make clean their hives very
carefully and kill their kings.

CHARLES ESTIENNE

Windy March

In the winds of windy March
   The catkins drop down
Curly, caterpillar-like,
   Curious, green and brown.

CHRISTINA ROSSETTI

March and April

In March and in April, from morning to night,
In sowing and setting good housewives delight
To have in a garden or other like plot
To trim up their houses, and furnish their pot.

THOMAS TUSSER

April! April!

April! April!
Laugh thy girlish laughter;
Then the moment after,
Weep thy girlish tears!

SIR WILLIAM WATSON

Aprille

When that Aprille with his shoures sote
The droghte of Marche hath perced to the rote.

GEOFFREY CHAUCER

May

Then came fair May,
The fairest mayd on ground
Dekt all with dainties of her season's pryde.

EDMUND SPENSER

May

Rough winds do shake the darling buds of May.

WILLIAM SHAKESPEARE

May is in his Prime

When May is in his prime, then may each heart rejoice:
When May bedecks each branch with green, each bird strains forth
    his voice.
The lively sap creeps up into the blooming thorn;
The flowers, which cold in prison kept, now laugh the frost to
    scorn.

All nature's imps triumph whiles joyful May doth last;
When May is gone, of all the year the pleasant time is past.

May makes the cheerful hue, May breeds and brings new blood;
May marcheth throughout every limb, May makes the merry mood.
May pricketh tender hearts their warbling notes to tune:
Full strange it is, yet some we see do make their May in June.
Thus things are strangely wrought whiles joyful May doth last;
Take May in time, when May is gone the pleasant time is past.

All ye that live on earth, and have your May at will,
Rejoice in May, as I do now, and use your May with skill.
Use May while that you may, for May hath but his time,
When all the fruit is gone, it is too late the tree to climb.
Your liking and your lust is fresh whiles May doth last;
When May is gone, of all the year the pleasant time is past.

RICHARD EDWARDS

Eight o'clock

The chestnut casts his flambeaux, and the flowers
    Stream from the hawthorn on the wind away.
The doors clap to, the pane is blind with showers.
    Pass me the can, lad; there's an end of May.

A E HOUSMAN

A Day in June

And what is so rare as a day in June?
    Then, if ever, come perfect days;
Then Heaven tries earth if it be in tune,
    And over it softly her warm ear lays.

J R LOWELL

The Rose

Whenas the mildest month
  Of jolly June doth spring,
And gardens green with happy hue
  Their famous fruits do bring,
When eke the lustiest time
  Reviveth youthly blood,
Then springs the finest featured flower
  In border fair that stood:
Which moveth me to say,
  In time of pleasant year,
Of all the pleasant flowers in June
  The red rose hath no peer.

THOMAS HOWELL

July

Then came hot July boiling like to fire.

EDMUND SPENSER

Gorgeous July

When all is said July is the most gorgeous of all the months,
especially in the garden. It is the one month of real summer that
is neither spring nor autumn.

ANON

The English Winter

The English winter—ending in July,
To recommence in August.

LORD BYRON

August Weather

Dead heat and windless air,
  And silence over all;
Never a leaf astir,
  But the ripe apples fall;
Plums are purple-red,
  Pears amber and brown;
Thud! in the garden-bed
  Ripe apples fall down.

Air like a cider-press
  With the bruised apples' scent;
Low whistles express
  Some sleepy bird's content;
Still world and windless sky,
  A mist of heat o'er all;
Peace like a lullaby,
  And the ripe apples fall.

KATHERINE TYNAN

September

September blow soft
'Til the fruit's in the loft.

THOMAS TUSSER

Brisk wind of September

In brisk wind of September
  The heavy-headed fruits
Shake upon their bending boughs
  And drop from their shoots.

CHRISTINA ROSSETTI

Variable October

The weather of October is usually distinguished by its variability, heavy rains, high winds and sharp frosts.

ANON

October

Bright October was come,
  The misty-eyed October.

A H CLOUGH

November

No sun—no moon
No morn—no noon
No dawn—no dusk
(No proper time of day)
No warmth, no cheerfulness, no healthful ease,
No comfortable feel in any member—
No shade, no shine, no bees,
No fruits, no flowers, no leaves, no birds—
  November!

THOMAS HOOD

November

November's sky is chill and drear,
November's leaf is red and sear.

SIR WALTER SCOTT

In a Drear-nighted December

In a drear-nighted December,
Too happy, happy Tree,
Thy branches ne'er remember
Their green felicity:
The north cannot undo them
With a sleety whistle through them,
Nor frozen thawings glue them
From budding at the prime.

In a drear-nighted December,
Too happy, happy Brook,
Thy bubblings ne'er remember
Apollo's summer look;
But with a sweet forgetting
They stay their crystal fretting,
Never, never petting
About the frozen time.

Ah would 'twere so with many
A gentle girl and boy!
But were there ever any
Writhed not at passéd joy?
To know the change and feel it,
When there is none to heal it
Nor numbéd sense to steal it—
Was never said in rhyme.

JOHN KEATS

Kecksies

I never think that the prospect of the garden in December is much
better by making all the flower-beds too tidy. I feel sure that the
dead flower-stems (the 'Kecksies' of Shakespeare and the old writers,
and the word still lingers in a few parts) must be some protection
to the plants; and, when the hoar-frosts come, these dead stems,
especially where the dead flower-heads remain, put on a wonderful
beauty, as any one may see who will walk by an old hedgerow in a
hoar-frost and look at the rank herbage, particularly where there is
any abundance of the large umbelliferous plants.

CANON HENRY ELLACOMBE

THE SEASONS

Spring's Delights

Spring's Delights are now returning!
  Let the Lazy Minstrel sing;
While the ruddy logs are burning,
  Let his merry banjo ring!
Take no heed of pluvial patter,
  Waste no time in vain regrets;
Though our teeth are all a-chatter
  Like the clinking castanets!
Though it's freezing, sleeting, snowing,
  Though we're speechless from catarrh,
Though the east wind's wildly blowing,
  Let us warble, *Tra-la-la*!

Spring's Delights are now returning!
  Let us order new great-coats:
Never let us dream of spurning
  Woollen wraps around our throats.
Let us see the couch nocturnal
  Snugly swathed in eider-down:
Let not thoughts of weather vernal
  Tempt us to go out of Town.
Though the biting blast is cruel,
  Though our 'tonic's' not *sol-fa*,
Though we sadly sup on gruel,
  Let us warble, *Tra-la-la*.

Spring's Delights are now returning!
  Now the poet deftly weaves
Quaint conceits and rhymes concerning
  Croton oil and mustard leaves!
Let us, though we are a fixture,
  In our room compelled to stay—
Let us quaff the glad cough mixture,
  Gaily gargle time away!
Though we're racked with pains rheumatic,
  Though to sleep we've said ta-ta,
Let us, with a voice ecstatic,
  Wildly warble, *Tra-la-la*!

Spring's Delights are now returning!
   Doctors now are blithe and gay!
Heaps of money now they're earning,
   Calls they're making ev'ry day.
Ev'ry shepherd swain grows colder,
   As, in vain, he tries to sing;
Feels he now quite ten years older
   'Neath the blast of blighting Spring!
Though we're doubtful of the issue,
   Let us bravely shout Hurrah!
And in one superb *A-tishoo*!
   Sneeze and warble, *Tra-la-la*

JOSEPH ASHBY STERRY

Spring Stops Me Suddenly

Spring stops me suddenly like ground
Glass under a door, squeaking and gibbering.
I put my hand to my cheek and the tips
Of my fingers feel blood pulsing and quivering.

A bud on a branch brushes the back
Of my hand and I look, without moving, down.
Summer is there, screwed and fused, compressed,
Neat as a bomb, its casing a dull brown.

From the window of a farther tree I hear
A chirp and a twitter; I blink.
A tow-headed vamp of a finch on a branch
Cocks a roving eye, tips me the wink

And, instantly, the whole great hot-lipped ensemble
Of birds and birds, of clay and glass doors,
Reels in with its ragtime chorus, staggering
The theme of the time, a jam-session's rattle and roar

With drums of summer jittering in the background
Dully and, deeper down and more human, the sobbing
Oboes of autumn falling across the track of the tune,
Winter's furtive bassoon like a sea-lion snorting and bobbing.

There is something here I do not get,
Some menace that I do not comprehend,
Yet, so intoxicating is the song,
I cannot follow its thought right to the end.

So up the garden path I go with Spring
Promising sacks and robes to rig my years
And a young girl to gladden my heart in a tartan
Scarf and freedom from my facile fears.

VALENTINE IREMONGER

Daffodils

Now the full-throated daffodils,
Our trumpeters in gold,
Call resurrection from the ground
And bid the year be bold.

Today the almond tree turns pink,
The first flush of the spring;
Winds loll and gossip through the town
Her secret whispering.

Now too the bird must try his voice
Upon the morning air;
Down drowsy avenues he cries
A novel great affair.

He tells of royalty to be;
How with her train of rose
Summer to coronation comes
Through waving wild hedgerows.

C DAY LEWIS

Spring

Spring, the sweet Spring, is the year's pleasant king;
Then blooms each thing, then maids dance in a ring,
Cold doth not sting, the pretty birds do sing—
     Cuckoo, jug-jug, pu-we, to-witta-woo!

The palm and may make country houses gay,
Lambs frisk and play, the shepherds pipe all day,
And we hear ay birds tune this merry lay—
     Cuckoo, jug-jug, pu-we, to-witta-woo!

The fields breathe sweet, the daisies kiss our feet,
Young lovers meet, old wives a-sunning sit,
In every street these tunes our ears do greet—
     Cuckoo, jug-jug, pu-we, to-witta-woo!
     Spring, the sweet Spring!

THOMAS NASHE

Summer

Summer has set in with its usual severity.

CHARLES LAMB

Sumer is icumen in

Sumer is icumen in,
     Llude sing cuccu!
Groweth sed, and bloweth med,
     And springeth the wude new.

ANON

Incomparable Summer

Italy has nothing like it, nor America. There never was such weather
except in England, where, in requital of a vast amount of horrible east
wind between February and June, and a brown October and black

November, and a wet, chill, sunless winter, there are a few weeks of incomparable summer, scattered through July and August, and the earlier portion of September, small in quantity, but exquisite enough to atone for the whole year's atmospherical delinquencies. After all, the prevalent sombreness may have brought out those sunny intervals in such high relief, that I see them, in my recollection, brighter than they really were: a little light makes a glory for people who live habitually in a gray gloom. The English, however, do not seem to know how enjoyable the momentary gleams of their summer are; they call it broiling weather, and hurry to the seaside with red, perspiring faces, in a state of combustion and deliquescence; and I have observed that even their cattle have similar susceptibilities, seeking the deepest shade, or standing mid-leg deep in pools and streams to cool themselves, at temperatures which our own cows would deem little more than barely comfortable. To myself, after the summer heats of my native land had somewhat effervesced out of my blood and memory, it was the weather of Paradise itself.

NATHANIEL HAWTHORNE

Drought

On the whole, after reckoning up all the losses and disappointments, I do not think that the gardener has much cause to complain of a long drought. There will be losses, of course, and so, perhaps, many gaps in the garden, but these we must expect every year from many causes, and the drought may teach us some good lessons. It teaches us very forcibly how steadily plant-life goes on in spite of all hindrances. It is really sad to go round the garden during a long drought, with the lawn brown, the shrubs getting scorched, and the beds looking almost like dust-heaps. Yet no sooner does the rain come than all is at once changed, and we are taught that the garden was by no means dead, but only biding its time; it was like a man who from illness or other cause is driven into enforced idleness, but who, as soon as the cause is removed, shows that the idleness was only from temporary weakness, which ended in increased strength. Within a very few days after the rains come to us after a long drought the grass becomes of the freshest green and the shrubs put out fresh leaves, herbaceous plants begin to shoot upwards, and it is no exaggeration to say that all Nature rejoices.

CANON HENRY ELLACOMBE

I Saw old Autumn

I saw old Autumn in the misty morn
Stand shadowless like silence, listening
To silence, for no lonely bird would sing
Into his hollow ear from woods forlorn,
Nor lowly hedge nor solitary thorn;
Shaking his languid locks all dewy bright
With tangled gossamer that fell by night,
  Pearling his coronet of golden corn.

THOMAS HOOD

Where Autumn Poises

Pause here awhile
Where autumn poises
On tawny foot
Before the long descent
Into the plain of winter.

Here the fruit swells
With joy along the branches;
The orchards blow
On scented horns of ripeness;
And the long grass

Strains upward,
Caresses curtseying apples,
Parting as they fall
Into deep jealous nests
In green recesses.

Walk with me here
Under laden branches,
Our faces brushing
The cheeks of apples,
Our fingers twisting

The dark lamps of plums
From their hanging places.
We will paint our lips
With wet blackberries
Among the last flowers,

The umbels of the tall
Angelica's flower-cities,
The final feathers of meadowsweet,
And watch September spiders
Hang out their hammocks.

FREDA LAUGHTON

Autumn Fires

In the other gardens
    And all up the vale,
From the autumn bonfires
    See the smoke trail!

Pleasant summer over
    And all the summer flowers,
The red fire blazes,
    The grey smoke towers.

Sing a song of seasons!
    Something bright in all!
Flowers in the summer,
    Fires in the fall!

ROBERT LOUIS STEVENSON

The Burning of the Leaves

Now is the time for the burning of the leaves.
They go to the fire; the nostril pricks with smoke
Wandering slowly into a seeping mist.
Brittle and blotched, ragged and rotten sheaves!
A flame seizes the smouldering ruin and bites
On stubborn stalks that crackle as they resist.

The last hollyhock's fallen tower is dust;
All the spices of June are a bitter reek,
All the extravagant riches spent and mean.
All burns! The reddest rose is a ghost;
Sparks whirl up, to expire in the mist: the wild
Fingers of fire are making corruption clean.

Now is the time for stripping the spirit bare,
Time for the burning of days ended and done,
Idle solace of things that have gone before:
Rootless hope and fruitless desire are there;
Let them go to the fire, with never a look behind.
The world that was ours is a world that is ours no more.

They will come again, the leaf and the flower, to arise
From squalor of rottenness into the old splendour,
And magical scents to a wondering memory bring;
The same glory, to shine upon different eyes.
Earth cares for her own ruins, naught for ours.
Nothing is certain, only the certain spring.

LAURENCE BINYON

Song

A spirit haunts the year's last hours
Dwelling amid these yellowing bowers:
    To himself he talks;
For at eventide, listening earnestly,
At his work you may hear him sob and
    sigh
      In the walks;

Earthward he boweth the heavy
   stalks
Of the mouldering flowers:
   Heavily hangs the broad sunflower
     Over its grave i'the earth so chilly;
   Heavily hangs the hollyhock,
     Heavily hangs the tiger-lily.

The air is damp, and hush'd, and close,
As a sick man's room when he taketh
   repose
     An hour before death;
My very heart faints and my whole soul
   grieves
At the moist rich smell of the rotting
   leaves,
     And the breath
     Of the fading edges of box beneath,
And the year's last rose.
   Heavily hangs the broad sunflower
     Over its grave i'the earth so chilly;
   Heavily hangs the hollyhock,
     Heavily hangs the tiger-lily.

ALFRED, LORD TENNYSON

FROM *Meditation in Winter*

I

In to thir dirk and drublie dayis,
Quhone sabill all the hewin arrayis,
   With mystie vapouris, cluddis and skyis,
   Nature all curage me denyis
Off sangis, ballattis, and of playis.

II

Quhone that the nycht dois lenthin houris,
With wind, with haill, and havy schouris,
   My dule spreit dois lurk for schoir;
   My hairt for languor dois forloir,
For laik of symmer with his flouris.

III

I walke, I turne, sleip may I nocht,
I vexit am with havy thocht;
   This warld all ouir I cast about,
   And ay the mair I am in dout,
The mair that I remeid have socht.

IV

I am assayit on everie syde,
Dispair sayis ay, 'In tyme prowyde,
   And get sum thing quhairon to leif;
   Or with grit trouble and mishcheif,
Thow sall in to this court abyde.'...

X

Yit, quhone the nycht begynnis to schort,
It dois my spreit sum pairt confort,
   Off thocht oppressit with the schouris.
   Cum, lustie symmer: with thy flouris,
That I may leif in sum disport.

                    Quod Dunbar.

                    WILLIAM DUNBAR

Nature at Work

All Nature seems at work. Slugs leave their lair—
   The bees are stirring—birds are on the wing—
And Winter slumbering in the open air
   Wears on his smilling face a dream of Spring!
And I the while, the sole unbusy thing,
Nor honey make, nor pair, nor build, nor sing.

              SAMUEL TAYLOR COLERIDGE

Winter Nights

Now winter nights enlarge
The number of their hours
And clouds their storms discharge
Upon the airy towers.

THOMAS CAMPION

Winter

I, singularly moved
To love the lovely that are not beloved,
Of all the Seasons, most
Love Winter.

COVENTRY PATMORE

THE WEATHER

When the Wind is in the East

When the wind is in the east,
'Tis neither good for man nor beast;
When the wind is in the north,
The skilful fisher goes not forth;
When the wind is in the south,
It blows the bait in the fishes' mouth;
When the wind is in the west,
Then 'tis at the very best.

ANON

Whether the Weather

Whether the weather be fine,
Or whether the weather be not;
Whether the weather be cold,
Or whether the weather be hot,
We'll weather the weather, whatever the weather,
Whether we like it or not.

OLD RHYME

Kissing

When gorse is not in bloom, kissing is out of season.

OLD SAYING

Contrasts and Diversities

The sublime is within the reach of few, the beautiful of many, for in
countries such as Italy and Britian the diversity of scenic loveliness
and local climate, of soil, rainfall and vegetation, is almost beyond

belief. In the north of Scotland there are gardens full of plants which at London would perish from the winter cold. In one Pembrokeshire valley the verbena is a tree of shade, while half a mile away there are shrivelled oaks in a waste of gorse and heather. At Brindisi, the traveller may shiver on the quay in a December wind, while summer is still reigning in the Consul's garden across the harbour mouth.

SIR GEORGE SITWELL

Weatherwise

Some are weather-wise, some are otherwise.

BENJAMIN FRANKLIN

The Hard Grey Weather

'Tis the hard grey weather
Breeds hard English men.

CHARLES KINGSLEY

Rain

It haint no use to grumble and complane
    It's jest as cheap and easy to rejoice;
When God sorts out the weather and sends rain.
    W'y rain's my choice.

JAMES WHITCOMB RILEY

Weathers

This is the weather the cuckoo likes,
    And so do I;
When showers betumble the chestnut spikes,
    And nestlings fly:

And the little brown nightingale bills his best,
And they sit outside at the 'Travellers' Rest',
And maids come forth sprig-muslin drest,
And citizens dream of the south and west,
   And so do I.

This is the weather the shepherd shuns,
   And so do I;
When beeches drip in browns and duns,
   And thresh, and ply;
And hill-hid tides throb, throe on throe,
And meadow rivulets overflow,
And drops on gate-bars hang in a row,
And rooks in families homeward go, .
   And so do I.

THOMAS HARDY

Kinds of Weather

There is really no such thing as bad weather, only different kinds of
good weather.

LORD AVEBURY

GARDENERS

The Character of a Skilful Gardener

He reaps the product of his labour'd ground.
His limes are first in flow'r, his lofty pines
With friendly shade secure his tender vines:
He ranks his elms in even graceful rows,
Is skill'd the grafted Pear-tree to dispose:
He makes with spreading planes a cool retreat,
To shade good fellows from the summer heat.

JOHN DRYDEN

Not For Adam Alone

He is a bad gardener whose garden is kept only for himself. Paradise
was not made for Adam only, but for 'every beast of the field and
every fowl of the air that was brought unto him' there. And we
add largely to the pleasure of our gardens when we look on them
not only as pleasant homes for our flowers and fruit, but also as the
homes of many lovely and interesting living creatures. We cannot
spare the birds, though we may have to pay largely for their beauty
and their song. We cannot spare the butterflies and moths, though
as caterpillars they are most destructive. I should be sorry not to
have the little spider which weaves such a net-work of beauty on
our shrubs in the early autumn mornings; and even our greatest
enemies, the slugs, snails and mice, which may be caught and
killed without mercy, add to the interest of our garden, and most
assuredly, though we may not see it, they have their use.

CANON HENRY ELLACOMBE

The Gardener's Bell

One of Andrew's acquaintance...happent to call, and the doctor told
him what ill socsess we had in our serch for the gardener's bell; upon
which he sought a sight of your yepissle, and read it as a thing that

was just wonderful for its whorsograffie, and then he sayid that, looking at the prinsipal of your spilling, he thought, we should read 'a gardener's bill or a list of flooring plants'; whilk being no doot your intent, I have proqurt the same, and it is includud heerin.

JOHN GALT

On Chosing a Gard'ner

I am for a *Gard'ner* that is neither too Old nor too Young; both Extreams being equally dangerous. Too much Youth is to be suspected of Ignorance and Wildness, and too much Age, unless supported by some Children of a reasonable Age and some Capacity, is subject to Laziness or Infirmity. Therefore, in my opinion, the best Age is from Twenty-five to Fifty and Fifty-five, carefully observing, whether the Face denotes any visible Appearance of Health, without any evaporated Brain, or foolish Presumption; likewise carefully chusing a Shape and Motion denoting a Sturdy, Vigorous, Nimble Man, not affecting to be dressed or adorn'd above the common Station of a Gard'ner.

JOHN EVELYN

Choosing a Gardener

An old lady's advice on choosing a gardener: 'Look at his trousers. If they're patched in the knees, you want him; if they're patched in the seat you don't.'

ANON

A Scotch Gardener's Tale

I have been upwards of fifty years in the line... I left Edinburgh in the year 1777, and, after working some time in Mr Christopher Gray's nursery, I got a very good place with a Mr Rolls, a great stockbroker, whose affairs went wrong after I had been six years with him, and I was obliged to quit. After going down to Scotland to see my friends, I came up again and got a place from Mr Hare, then a seedsman in St James's Street, to go to Mrs Wilson at Putney, where I remained until her daughter married, when, her husband having an aversion to Scotch servants, I was obliged to leave. Soon after this a fellow workman and myself attempted to set up a small nursery at Epsom...but after struggling hard for little more than two years, we were obliged to give up, after losing all we have saved and almost £50, which my partner had borrowed from his aunt at Kinross...

Not liking to go into servitude again, I began jobbing on my own account, and a poor business I have found it ever since. When I first began, the highest wages I could get were 3s. a day, and obliged to find my own tools. I had a good deal of employment at first, partly from the circumstances of being a Scotchman...

My wife also took up a greengrocer's shop about this time, and we did very well until we lost our only daughter, which obliged us to take in a maid-servant, who let some fellows into the house one Sunday afternoon when we were at chapel and they took away all my savings...

After doing nothing for some time, I began jobbing again at Paddington, and my wife took in washing; but she falling ill, we removed to Hackney, on account of the air, where I have been ever since, being just able to gain a livelihood, by laying out the gardens of the new buildings going on in the neighbourhood.

ARCHIBALD McNAUGHTON

Old Gardener

I kneel down painfully and touch the dirty lace
Of cabbage leaves, all crinkled like my face
And preying hands, twisted, but still able
To pluck out weeds between the vegetables
And give them space freely to suck and chew
The soil their muscular stalks stick through.

Fifty years I've filled boxes for market
For men to buy and eat, digest and defecate.
The roar of teeth clashing fills my inner
Ear. The world is always at dinner.
I hear the jaws of caterpillars ravage
The thick leaves of the hungry cabbage.

Older, weaker, never to be fatter,
I am frightened of chewing, chewing, chewing. Matter
Is eating matter, and I, who buy and sell
And nurture ravagers, am chewed as well,
Living between Jehovah's jaws until
The garden is empty and his grinders are still.

JAMES SIMMONS

The Work of Your Owne Hands

View now with delight the works of your owne hands, your fruit trees of all sorts, loaden with sweet blossomes, and fruit of all tasts, operations, and coloures; your trees standing in comely order which way soever you looke.

Your borders on every side hanging and drooping with Feberries, Raspberries, Barberries, Currens, and the roots of your trees powdred with Strawberries, red, white and greene, what a pleasure is this?

Your Gardiner can frame your lesser wood to the shape of men armed in the field, ready to give battell: or swift running Grey hounds: or of well sented and true running Hounds, to chase the Deere, or hunt the Hare. This kinde of hunting shall not waste your corne, nor much your coyne.

Mazes well framed a man's height, may perhaps make your friend wander in gathering of berries, till he cannot recover himselfe without your helpe.

To have occasion to Exercise within your Orchard: it shall be a pleasure to have a Bowling Alley, or rather (which is more manly, and more healthfull) a payre of Buttes, to stretch your armes.

THOMAS HILL

A River of Petals

These apple-trees, which Iden had planted, flung sackfuls of bloom at his feet. They poured themselves out in abandoned, open-armed, spendthrift, wasteful—perfectly prodigal—quantities of rose-tinted petal; prodigal as a river which flows full to the brim, never questioning but what there will be plenty of water to follow.

Flowers, and trees, and grass seemed to spring up wherever Iden set down his foot: fruit and flowers fell from the air down upon him. It was his genius to make things grow—like sunshine and shower; a sort of Pan, a half-god of leaves and boughs, and reeds and streams, a sort of Nature in human shape, moving about and sowing Plenty and Beauty.

One side of the summer-house was a thick holly-bush, Iden had set it there; he builded the summer-house and set the ivy; and the pippin at the back, whose bloom was white, the copper-birch nearby; the great sycamore alone had been there before him, but he set a seat under it, and got woodbine to flower there; the drooping ash he planted, and if Amaryllis stood under it when the tree was in full leaf you could not see her, it made so complete an arbour; the Spanish oak in the corner; the box-hedge along the ha-ha carpet; the red currants against the red wall; the big peony yonder; the damsons and pear; the yellow honeybush; all these, and this was but one square, one mosaic of the garden, half of it sward, too, and besides these there was the rhubarb patch at one corner; fruit, flowers, plants and herbs, lavender, parsley, which has a very pleasant green, growing in a thick bunch, roses, pale sage—read Boccacio and the sad story of the leaf-sage—ask Nature if you wish to know how many things more there were.

RICHARD JEFFERIES

The Old Gardener

In the Italian Garden
tulips iris wait
for the old bent gardener
to open the heavy gate.

Down the flagged steps he dodders,
and fills his watering-can,
making the water-lilies
sway—the clumsy old man.

When he was young the gardener
had sterner tasks than this;
now he waters at morning
tulips and irises

HUMBERT WOLFE

Considering and Composing

It always seems to me that one of the things most worth doing about
a garden is to try to make every part of it beautiful...And to get
into the habit of considering and composing...arrangements, and to
worry out the way of doing them, is by no means one of the least of
the pleasures of a garden.

GERTRUDE JEKYLL

Women Gardeners

The excuses which women make for their gardens, when you are
visiting them, are as nothing to the stories they invent about them
when you are a safe hundred miles away. If you sit next to a woman
gardener at dinner, she will have given you the impression, before
the butler has refilled her glass, that though she lives in Surrey, her
garden is an Arabian Nights fantasy of beauty. You would think that
she could hardly walk through the rose garden because the standards
are so prolific with buds, or that she must be sent into a nightly
stupour by the fumes of her quite phenomenal wistaria. Everything,
according to her account, 'grows like a weed—my dear—really like a
weed.'

BEVERLEY NICHOLS

British Gardeners

British Gardeners, instead of humouring Nature, love to deviate
from it as much as possible. Our trees rise in Cones, Globes and
Pyramids. We see the marks of scissors upon every Plant and Bush.

I do not know whether I am singular in my opinion, but, for my own part, I would rather look upon a tree in all its Luxuriancy and Diffusion of Boughs and Branches, than when it is thus cut and trimmed into a Mathematical Figure, and cannot but fancy that an Orchard in Flower looks infinitely more delightful than all the little Labyrinths of the most finished Parterre...I have always thought a kitchen garden a more pleasant sight than the finest orangery...I love to see everything in perfection, and am more pleased to survey my rows of coleworts and cabbages, with a thousand nameless pot herbs springing up in their full fragrancy and verdure, than to see the tender plants of foreign countries.

JOSEPH ADDISON

Capability Brown

Improvement too, the idol of the age,
Is fed with many a victim. Lo, he comes!
Th'omnipotent magician, Brown, appears!
Down falls the venerable pile, th'abode
Of our forefathers—a grave whisker'd race,
But tasteless. Springs a palace in its stead,
But in a distant spot; where, more expos'd,
It may enjoy th'advantage of the north,
And aguish east, till time shall have transform'd
Those naked acres to a shelt'ring grove.
He speaks. The lake in front becomes a lawn;
Woods vanish, hills subside, and valleys rise:
And streams, as if created for his use,
Pursue the track of his directing wand,
Sinuous or straight, now rapid and now slow,
Now murm'ring soft, now roaring in cascades—
Ev'n as he bids! Th'enraptur'd owner smiles.
'Tis finish'd, and yet, finish'd as it seems,
Still wants a grace, the loveliest it could show,
A mine to satisfy th'enormous cost.
Drain'd to the last poor item of his wealth,
He sighs, departs, and leaves th'accomplish'd plan
That he has touch'd, retouch'd, many a long day
Labour'd, and many a night pursu'd in dreams,

Just when it meets his hopes, and proves the heav'n
He wanted, for a wealthier to enjoy!

WILLIAM COWPER

On Capability Brown

So closely did he copy nature that his works will be mistaken.

ANON

More Capability

We were standing on a terrace at Blenheim Palace admiring the view with many other tourists, when a large American lady with an equally large voice declared: 'Isn't it beautiful? Of course, you know, it was designed by Capability Smith.'

MARY L PERKINS

A Room on a Garden

O stagnant east-wind, palsied mare,
Giddap! The ruby roses' hair
Must blow.

Behold how order is the end
Of everything. The roses bend
As one.

Order, the law of hoes and rakes,
May be perceived in windy quakes
And squalls.

The gardener searches earth and sky
The truth in nature to espy
In vain.

He well might find that eager balm
In lilies' stately-statued calm;
But then

He well might find it in this fret
Of lilies rusted, rotting, wet
With rain.

WALLACE STEVENS

Painting Tulips

A large rose-tree stood near the entrance of the garden: the roses
growing on it were white, but there were three gardeners at it, busily
painting them red. Alice thought this a very curious thing, and she
went nearer to watch them, and just as she came up to them she
heard one of them say 'Look out now, Five! Don't go splashing paint
over me like that!'
     'I couldn't help it,' said Five, in a sulky tone.
'Seven jogged my elbow.'
     On which Seven looked up and said 'That's right, Five! Always lay
the blame on others!'
     '*You'd* better not talk!' said Five. 'I heard the Queen say only
yesterday you deserved to be beheaded!'
     'What for?' said the one who had first spoken.
     'That's none of *your* business, Two!' said Seven.
     'Yes, it is his business!' said Five. 'And I'll tell him—it was for
bringing the cook tulip roots instead of onions.'
     Seven flung down his brush, and had just begun 'Well, of all the
unjust things—' when his eye chanced to fall upon Alice, as she
stood watching them, and he checked himself suddenly: the others
looked round also, and all of them bowed low.
     'Would you tell me,' said Alice, a little timidly, 'why you are
painting these roses?'
     Five and Seven said nothing, but looked at Two. Two began in a
low voice, 'Why, the fact is, you see, Miss, this here ought to have
been a *red* rose-tree, and we put a white one in by mistake; and if the
Queen was to find it out, we should all have our heads cut off, you
know. So you see, Miss, we're doing our best, afore she comes, to—'
At this moment, Five, who had been anxiously looking across the
garden, called out 'The Queen! The Queen!' and the three gardeners

instantly threw themselves flat upon their faces. There was a sound of many footsteps, and Alice looked round, eager to see the Queen.

LEWIS CARROLL

The Last Clean Bough

Each day that summer he walked the avenue
of elm and hawthorn to the broken orchard.

He put his saw to the dry bough and he thought
of autumns full of fruit, of blossomings.

And he remembered a girl, a night when leaves
moved in the wind and moonlight silvered her.

But that was fifty years ago...Now
the house beyond the orchard was a shell.

The orchard wall had fallen stone by stone
and the fruitless trees had fallen: apple, plum,

damson, cherry, pear—the pear tree where
the summer moon had found the silver girl.

The girl beneath the tree beneath the moon
was long since dead. What had they said

that summer night beneath the pear tree where
now he put his saw to the last clean bough?

He shouldered the branch and walked the avenue
of big elms and sparse hawthorn hedge.

In his garden he dropped it on the pile
of timbers stacked against the coming frost.

JAMES AITCHISON

How to Cover the Ground

One autumn, a jobbing gardener and I
dug over a lady's suburban garden.
When we finished, he looked at the dark clods
and said, with satisfaction,
That's the way I like to see it—
none o' they bloody flowers.

NORMAN MacCAIG

Treasures

I overheard two lavender-scented old ladies on Fellows' Day at the
Chelsea Flower Show. One said to the other:

'Now my head gardener is dead, I'll be able to let you have some
treasures from the greenhouse.'

MRS W P BUXTON

The Florist

In innocence, purity, and simplicity the florist—not the scientific
botanist, but the florist of his own little borders, is the only rival of
the angler. I wish we had a good Flowery Walton.

LORD COCKBURN

The Broken-Hearted Gardener

I'm a broken-hearted Gardener, and don't know what to do,
My love she is inconstant, and a fickle jade, too,
One smile from her lips will never be forgot,
It refreshes, like a shower from a watering pot.

CHORUS
Oh, Oh! she's a fickle wild rose,
A damask, a cabbage, a young China rose.

She's my myrtle, my geranium,
My Sunflower, my sweet marjorum,
My honey suckle, my tulip, my violet,
My hollyhock, my dahlia, my mignonette.

We grew up together like two apple trees,
And clung to each other like double sweet peas,
Now they're going to trim her, and plant her in a pot,
And I'm left to wither, neglected and forgot.

She's my snowdrop, my ranunculus,
My hyacinth, my gilliflower, my polyanthus,
My heart's ease, my pink, water lily,
My buttercup, my daisy, my daffydown dilly.

I'm like a scarlet runner that has lost its stick,
Or a cherry that's left for the dickey to pick,
Like a waterpot, I weep, like a paviour I sigh,
Like a mushroom I'll wither, like a cucumber, die.

I'm like a humble bee that doesn't know where to settle,
And she'a dandelion, and a stinging nettle,
My heart's like a beet choked with chickweed,
And my head's like a pumpkin running to seed.

I'm a great mind to make myself a felo-de-se,
And finish all my woes on the branch of a tree,
But I won't for I know at my kicking, you'd roar,
And honour my death with a double encore.

ANON

A Garden Song

I scorn the doubts and cares that hurt
    The world and all its mockeries,
My only care is not to squirt
    The ferns among my rockeries.

In early youth and later life
    I've seen an up and seen a down,

And now I have a loving wife
  To help me peg verbena down.

Of joys that come to womankind
  The loom of fate doth weave her few,
But here are summer joys entwined
  And bound with golden feverfew.

I've learnt the lessons one and all
  With which the world its sermon stocks,
Now, heedless of a rise or fall,
  I've Brompton and I've German stocks.

In peace and quiet pass our days,
  With nought to vex our craniums
Our middle beds are all ablaze
  With red and white geraniums.

And like a boy I laugh when she,
  In Varden hat and Varden hose,
Comes slyly up the lawn at me
  To squirt me with the garden hose.

Let him who'd have the peace he needs
  Give all his worldly mumming up,
Then dig a garden, plant the seeds,
  To watch the product coming up.

                                GEORGE R SIMS

The Planting of the Vine

When Noah first planted the Vine,
  The Devil contrived to be there,
For he saw pretty well that the finding of Wine
  Was a very important affair.

Mankind had been sober before;
  But had *not* been particularly good;
And the cold-blooded crew had deserved all the more
  To be deluged and drenched by the Flood.

Then the grape came to gladden man's heart;
  And a bright dawn of bliss seemed to glow,
When the rainbow and wine-cup could tidings impart,
  Of an end both to Water and Woe.

ANON

To a Gardener

FRIEND, in my mountain-side demesne,
My plain-beholding, rosy, green
And linnet-haunted garden-ground,
Let still the esculents abound.
Let first the onion flourish there,
Rose among roots, the maiden-fair,
Wine-scented and poetic soul
Of the capacious salad bowl.
Let thyme the mountaineer(to dress
The tinier birds) and wading cress,
The lover of the shallow brook,
From all my plots and borders look.
Nor crisp and ruddy radish, nor
Pease-cods for the child's pinafore
Be lacking; nor of salad clan
The last and least that ever ran
About great nature's garden-beds.
Nor thence be missed the speary heads
Of artichoke; nor thence the bean
That gathered innocent and green
Outsavours the belauded pea.

These tend, I prithee; and for me,
Thy most long-suffering master, bring
In April, when the linnets sing
And the days lengthen more and more
At sundown to the garden door.
And I, being provided thus,
Shall, with superb asparagus,
A book, a taper, and a cup
Of country wine, divinely sup.

ROBERT LOUIS STEVENSON

The Misfortunate Gardener

Seeds are sowing in some parts where plants ought to be reaping, and plants are running to seed while they are thought not yet at maturity. Our garden, therefore, is not yet quite the most profitable thing in the world; but Mr d'A assures me it is to be the staff of our table and existence.

A little, too, he has been unfortunate; for, after immense toil in planting and transplanting strawberries round our hedge, here at Bookham, he has just been informed they will bear no fruit the first year, and the second we may be 'over the hills and far away!'

Another time, too, with great labour, he cleared a considerable compartment of weeds, and when it looked clean and well, and he showed his work to the gardener, the man said he had demolished an asparagus bed! M d'A protested, however, nothing could look more like *les mauvaises herbes*.

His greatest passion is for transplanting. Everything we possess he moves from one end of the garden to another, to produce better effects. Roses take place of jessamines, jessamines of honeysuckles, and honeysuckles of lilacs, till they have all danced round as far as the space allows...

Such is our horticultural history. But I must not omit that we have had for one week cabbages from our own cultivation every day! Oh, you have no idea how sweet they tasted! We agreed they had a freshness and a *goût* we had never met before. We had them for too short a time to grow tired of them, because, as I have already hinted, they were beginning to run to seed before we knew they were eatable....

M d'Arblay has worked most laboriously in his garden, but his misfortunes there, during our absence, might melt a heart of stone. The horses of our neighbouring farmer broke through our hedges, and have made a kind of bog of our meadow, by scampering in it during the wet; the sheep followed, who have eaten up all our greens, every sprout and cabbage and lettuce destined for the winter, while the horses dug up our turnips and carrots; and the swine, pursuing such examples, have trod down all the young plants, besides devouring whatever the others left of vegetables. Our potatoes, left, from our abrupt departure, in the ground, are all rotten or frost-bitten, and utterly spoilt; and not a single thing has our whole ground produced us since we came home. A few dried carrots, which remain from the indoor collection, are all we have to temper our viands.

FANNY BURNEY

For Bonfires

The leaves are gathered, the trees are dying
for a time.
A seagull cries through white smoke in the garden fires
that fill the heavy air.
All day heavy air
is burning, a moody dog
sniffs and circles the swish of the rake.
In streaks of ash, the gardener drifting
ghostly, beats his hands, a cloud
of breath to the red sun.

EDWIN MORGAN

Burning the Leaves

This was the first day that the leaves
Came down in hordes, in hosts, a great wealth
Gambled away over the green lawn
Belonging to the house, old fry and spawn
Of the rich year converted into filth
In the beds by the wall, the gutters under the eaves.
We thought of all the generations gone
Like that, flyers, migrants, fugitives.

We come like croupiers with rakes,
To a bamboo clatter drag these winnings in,
Our windfall, firstfruits, tithes and early dead
Fallen on our holdings from overhead,
And taxable to trees against our sin.
Money to burn! We play for higher stakes
Than the mere leaves, and, burdened with treasure, tread
The orbit of the tree that heaven shakes.

The wrath of God we gather up today,
But not for long. In the beginning night
We light our hoarded leaves, the flames arise,
The smell of smoke takes memory by surprise,
And we become as children in our sight.
That is, I think, the object of this play,
Though our children dance about the sacrifice
Unthinking, their shadows lengthened and cast away.

HOWARD NEMEROV

BIRDSONG

A Richness of Musical Sound

A place to eat and drink, and think of nothing in, listening to the goldfinches, and watching them carry up the moss, and lichen, and slender fibres for their nest in the fork of the apple; listening to the swallows as they twittered past, or stayed on the sharp, high top of the pear tree, to the vehement starlings, whistling and screeching like Mrs Iden herself, on the chimneys; chaffinches 'chink, chink', thrushes, distant blackbirds, who like oaks: 'cuckoo, cuckoo,' 'crake, crake,' buzzing and burring of bees, coo of turtle-doves, now and then a neigh, to remind you that there were horses, fulness and richness of musical sound; a world of grass and leaf, humming like a hive with voices.

RICHARD JEFFERIES

Fruit for their Songs

There is another circumstance in which I am very particular, or, as my neighbours call me, very whimsical; as my garden invites into it all the birds of the country, by offering them the conveniency of springs and shades, solitude and shelter, I do not suffer any one to destroy their nests in the Spring, or drive them from their usual haunts in fruit-time; I value my garden more for being full of blackbirds than cherries, and very frankly give them fruit for their songs. By this means I have always the music of the season in its perfection, and am highly delighted to see the jay or the thrush hopping about my walks, and shooting before my eye across the several little glades and alleys that I pass through.

JOSEPH ADDISON

Nightingales, Alpes, Finches

In many places were nightingales,
Alpes, finches, and wodewales,
That in her swete song delyten
In thilke place as they habyten.

Ther mighte men see many flokkes
Of turtles and of laverokkes.
Chalaundres fele saw I there,
That wery, nigh forsongen were.
And thrustles, terins, and mavys,
That songen for to winne hem prys,
And eek to sormounte in hir song
These other briddes hem among.
By note made fair servyse
These briddes, that I you devyse;
They songe hir song as faire and well
As angels doon espirituel.
Swich swete song was hem among,
That me thoughte it no briddes song,
But it was wonder lyk to be
Song of mermaydens of the see;
That, for her singing is so clere,
Though we mermaydens clepe hem here
In English, as in our usaunce,
Men clepen hem sereyns in Fraunce.

GUILLAUME DE LORIS

Ripe Strawberries

My strawberries now ripe and the better for being layered into casks pierced with holes from which they sprout and hang down in garlands, a pretty sight, but O the blackbirds and thrushes do often prevail against nets, though I set springes against them of horsehair. Yet the birds are my gardeners against the pest of insects, grubs, caterpillars, and all manner of small things, so I do balance a pecked strawberry against small slugs.

DION CLAYTON CALTHROP

Different Answers

If I were to ask the question whether birds were useful or harmful in the garden, I should get many different answers. The professional gardener would answer, without any hesitation, that he would be glad to have them all cleared away. And certainly it is a vexing thing to have to wage constant war with them, from the sowing of the seed till the crops are gathered, and generally to be beaten by them, for most of them have no respect for gardeners, and no fear of any sort of scarecrows, or if they ever have a fear, a very short acquaintance with the scarecrow soon breeds contempt, and they use it for a point of vantage. Yet there is much to be said for the birds, even from the gardener's point of view.

CANON HENRY ELLACOMBE

Waggletail

Out rins Waggletail
Cheep, cheep, chitterin,
Jinkin owre the dewy grass
And spurtlin up a spetterin.

Bobbin here, bobbin there,
Fliskerin and flitterin;
Jinkin owre the dewy grass
Wi' his leggies whitterin.

WILLIAM SOUTAR

Yellow Yorlins

Three yorlins flitter'd frae the elder tree;
Three glisterin yorlins gledsome on the e'e:
Pity the blind folk, wha hae never seen
The yellow yorlin, for they canna ken
Sae sma' a sicht is a' a man need hae
To keep his hert abüne its misery.

WILLIAM SOUTAR

A Broode of Nightingales

A broode of Nightingales, who with their several notes and tunes, with a strong delightsome voyce, out of a weake body, will beare you company night and day. She loves (and lives in) hots of wood in her heart. She will help you to cleanse your trees of Caterpillars, and all noysome wormes and flyes. The gentle Robbin-red-brest will helpe her, and in Winter in the coldest stormes will keepe a part.

Neither will the Silly Wren be behind in Summer, with her distinct whistle (like a sweet Recorder) to cheere your spirits.

The Black-bird and Threstle (for I take it the Thrush sings not, but devoures) sing loudly in a May morning, and delights the Eare much (and you neede not want their company, if you have ripe Cherryes or Berries, and would as gladly as the rest doe you pleasure:) but I had rather want their company than my fruit.

THOMAS HILL

Birds' Lament

Oh, says the linnet, if I sing,
My love forsook me in the spring,
And nevermore will I be seen
Without my satin gown of green.

Oh, says the pretty-feathered jay,
Now my love is fled away
For the memory of my dear
A feather of each sort I'll wear.

Oh, says the sparrow, my love is gone,
She so much that I doted on,
And e'er since for that selfsame thing
I've made a vow I ne'er will sing.

Oh, says the water-wag-my-tail,
I courted a fair one but could not prevail,
I could not with my love prevail,
So that is the reason I wag my tail.

Oh, says the pretty speckled thrush,
That changes its note from bush to bush,
My love has left me here alone
And I fear she never will return.

Oh, says the rook, and eke the crow,
The reason why in black we go—
Because our love has us forsook,
So pity us, poor crow and rook.

Oh, says the owl, my love is gone,
It was her I doted on;
Since she has gone I know not where to follow,
But after her I'll whoop and hollo.

JOHN CLARE

Robins

Reminder of a world not of our making,
They have their own greeting,
Their own weeping,
Their privacy, custom and formality.

Winter compels their beggary at our doors,
But they as in court dress,
Stiff with apprehensive elegance,
Present to us their note for maintenance.

GEORGE BRUCE

A Sparrow

I once had a sparrow alight upon my shoulder, for a moment
while I was hoeing in a village garden, and I felt that I was more
distinguished by that circumstance than I should have been by any
epaulet I could have worn.

HENRY DAVID THOREAU

Sparrow and Robin

Merry Merry Sparrow,
Under leaves so green,
A happy Blossom
Sees you swift as arrow
Seek your cradle narrow
Near my bosom.

Pretty Pretty Robin
Under leaves so green,
Hears you sobbing, sobbing,
Pretty Pretty Robin
Near my bosom.

WILLIAM BLAKE

The Thrush's Nest

Within a thick and spreading hawthorn bush
    That overhung a mole-hill large and round,
I heard from morn to morn a merry thrush
    Sing hymns to sunrise, and I drank the sound
With joy; and, often an intruding guest,
    I watched her secret toils from day to day—
How true she warped the moss to form a nest,
    And modelled it within the wood and clay;
And by and by, like heath-bells gilt with dew,
    There lay her shining eggs, as bright as flowers,
Ink-spotted over shells of greeny blue;
    And there I witnessed, in the sunny hours,
A brood of nature's minstrels chirp and fly,
    Glad as that sunshine and the laughing sky.

JOHN CLARE

A Thrush

Just below...lay the lawn, garlanded round with sleeping and dew-drenched flower-beds, and the incense of their fragrant buds and folded petals still slept in the censer, till in the east should rise the gold-haired priest, and swing it, tossing high to heaven the sweetness of its burning. And then from out of the bushes beyond there scudded a thrush...He scurried over the shimmering lawn with innumerable footfalls...Then he swelled his throat, and sang one soft phrase of morning, paused as if listening, and repeated it. All the magic of youth and joy of life were there...Another voice, and yet another, sounded from the bushes; there were other thrushes there, and in the ivy of the house arose the cheerful jangling of sparrows. Fresh feathered forms ran out on to the lawn, and the air was shrill with their pipings. Every moment the sky grew brighter with the imminent day, the last star faded in the glow of pink translucent alabaster, and in the green-crowned elms the breeze of morning awoke and stirred the tree-tops. Then it came lower, and began to move in the flower-beds, and the wine of the dew was spilled from the chalices of new-blown roses, and the tall lilies quivered.

E F BENSON

Through Field-Glasses

Though buds still speak in hints
And frozen ground has set the flints
As fast as precious stones
And birds perch on the boughs, silent as cones,

Suddenly waked from sloth
Young trees put on a ten years' growth
And stones double their size,
Drawn nearer through field-glasses' greater eyes.

Why I borrow their sight
Is not to give small birds a fright
Creeping up close by inches;
I make the trees come, bringing tits and finches.

I lift a field itself
As lightly as I might a shelf,
And the rooks do not rage
Caught for a moment in my crystal cage.

And while I stand and look,
Their private lives an open book,
I feel so privileged
My shoulders prick, as though they were half fledged.

ANDREW YOUNG

Two Birds

A single note, the cuckoo's, in the spring.
Hidden in the woods, it sends its greeting.
We are shaken wildly by the usual thing,
the possibility of a fertile meeting.

And we remember how the redbreast came
as far as the lobby with its slanted head
and how we read in some laborious tome
that after a year the little bird is dead.

IAIN CRICHTON SMITH

Fragment

REPEAT that, repeat,
Cuckoo, bird, and open ear wells, heart-springs, delightfully sweet,
With a ballad, with a ballad, a rebound
Off trundled timber and scoops of the hillside ground,
    hollow hollow hollow ground:
The whole landscape flushes on a sudden at a sound.

GERARD MANLEY HOPKINS

Spring's Welcome

What bird so sings, yet so does wail?
O 'tis the ravish'd nightingale.
Jug, jug, jug, jug, tereu! she cries,
And still her woes at midnight rise.
Brave prick-song! Who is 't now we hear?
None but the lark so shrill and clear;
How at heaven's gates she claps her wings,
The morn not waking till she sings.
Hark, hark, with what a pretty throat
Poor robin redbreast tunes his note!
Hark how the jolly cuckoos sing
Cuckoo! to welcome in the spring!
Cuckoo! to welcome in the spring!

JOHN LYLY

I Watched a Blackbird

I watched a blackbird on a budding sycamore
One Easter Day, when sap was stirring twigs to the core;
  I saw his tongue, and crocus-coloured bill
  Parting and closing as he turned his trill;
  Then he flew down, seized on a stem of hay,
And upped to where his building scheme was under way,
As if so sure a nest were never shaped on spray.

THOMAS HARDY

Starling On a Green Lawn

He makes such a business of going somewhere
he's like a hopping with a bird in it.

The somewhere's an any place, which he recognises at once.
His track is zig-zagzigzag- zag.

He angles himself to the sun and his blackness
becomes something fallen from a stained-glass window.

He's a guy King, a guy Prince, though his only royal habit
is to walk with his hands clasped behind his back.

Now he's flown up like a mad glove on to a fence post.
He squinnies at the world and draws a cork from a bottle.

NORMAN MacCAIG

Goldfinches

Sometimes goldfinches one by one will drop
From low hung branches; little space they stop,
But sip, and twitter, and their feathers sleek;
Then off at once, as in a wanton freak,
Or perhaps, to show their black and golden wings,
Pausing upon their yellow flutterings.

JOHN KEATS

Birdsongs

The ousel-cock, so black of hue,
    With orange-tawny bill,
The throstle with his note so true,
    The wren with little quill;
The finch, the sparrow, and the lark,
    The plain-song cuckoo gray,
Whose note full many a man doth mark,
    And dare not answer nay.

WILLIAM SHAKESPEARE

Proud Songsters

The thrushes sing as the sun is going,
    And the finches whistle in ones and pairs,
And as it gets dark loud nightingales
    In bushes
Peep, as they can when April wears,
    As if all time were theirs.

These are brand-new birds of twelve-months' growing,
Which a year ago, or less than twain,
No finches were, nor nightingales,
    Nor thrushes,
But only particles of grain,
    And earth, and air, and rain.

THOMAS HARDY

The Siskins

The bank swallows veer and dip,
Diving down at my windows,
Then flying almost straight upward,
Like bats in daytime,
And their shadows, bigger,
Race over the thick grass;
And the finches pitch through the air, twittering;
And the small mad siskins flit by,
Flying upward in little skips and erratic leaps;
Or they sit sideways on limber dandelion stems,
Bending them down to the ground;
Or perch and peck at larger flower-crowns,
Springing, one to another,
The last abandoned stalk always quivering
Back into straightness;
Or they fling themselves against tree trunks,
Scuttling down and around like young squirrels,
Birds furious as bees.

Now they move all together!—
These airy hippety-hop skippers,
Light as seed blowing off thistles!
And I seem to lean forward,
As my eyes follow after
Their sunlit leaping.

THEODORE ROETHKE

The Birds

They leave us always in the autumn when
the fields are stubbly, and the sun is low.
They seek the south: we in the north must grow
older and wiser till they return again

instinctive, loveable and superficial,
whistlers of the spring, for that's their strength
that however much the days are drawn in length
they have learned nothing new: or chosen special

bushes to sing from with their trembling blossoms
on mornings of the future or the past
but only the present on which they are cast
and do not see wild winter's broken chasms.

IAIN CRICHTON SMITH

Bridal Song

Roses, their sharp spines being gone,
Not royal in their smells alone,
    But in their hue;
Maiden pinks, of odour faint,
Daisies smell-less, yet most quaint,
    And sweet thyme true;
Primrose, firstborn child of Ver,
Merry springtime's harbinger,
    With her bells dim;

Oxlips in their cradles growing,
Marigold on death-beds blowing,
   Larks'-heels trim—
All dear Nature's children sweet,
Lie 'fore bride and bridegroom's feet
   Blessing their sense.

Not an angel of the air,
Bird melodious, or bird fair,
   Is absent hence.
The crow, the slanderous cuckoo, nor
The boding raven, nor chough hoar,
   Nor chattering pie,
May on our bride-house perch or sing,
Or with them any discord bring,
   But from it fly.

WILLIAM SHAKESPEARE(?)

A Bird Came Down the Walk

A Bird came down the Walk—
He did not know I saw—
He bit an Angleworm in halves
And ate the fellow, raw,

And then he drank a Dew
From a convenient Grass—
And then hopped sidewise to the Wall
To let a Beetle pass—

He glanced with rapid eyes
That hurried all around—
They looked like frightened Beads, I thought—
He stirred his Velvet Head

Like one in danger, Cautious,
I offered him a Crumb,
and he unrolled his feathers
And rowed him softer home—

Than Oars divide the Ocean,
Too silver for a seam—
Or Butterflies, off Banks of Noon
Leap, plashless as they swim.

EMILY DICKINSON

Birds

SURE maybe ye've heard the storm-thrush
    Whistlin' bould in March,
Before there's a primrose peepin' out,
    Or a wee red cone on the larch;
Whistlin' the sun to come out o' the cloud,
    An' the wind to come over the sea,
But for all he can whistle so clear an' loud,
    He's never the bird for me.

Sure maybe ye've seen the song-thrush
    After an April rain
Slip from in-undher the drippin' leaves,
    Wishful to sing again;
An' low wi' love when he's near the nest,
    An' loud from the top of the tree,
But for all he can flutter the heart in your breast,
    He's never the bird for me.

Sure maybe ye've heard the cushadoo
    Callin' his mate in May,
When one sweet thought is the whole of his life,
    An' he tells it the one sweet way.
But my heart is sore at the cushadoo
    Filled wid his own soft glee,
Over an' over his 'me an' you!'
    He's never the bird for me.

Sure maybe ye've heard the red-breast
    Singin' his lone on a thorn,
Mindin' himself o' the dear days lost,
    Brave wid his heart forlorn.
The time is in dark November,

An' no spring hopes has he:
'Remember,' he sings, 'remember!'
Ay, *thon's* the wee bird for me.

MOIRA O'NEILL

The Arrival of the Mocking-Bird

I sincerely congratulate you on the arrival of the mocking bird. Learn all the children to venerate it as a superior being in the form of a bird, or as a being which will haunt them if any harm is done to itself or its eggs. I shall hope that the multiplication of the cedar in the neighbourhood, and of tree and shrubs round the house, could attract more of them; for they like to be in the neighbourhood of our habitations if they furnish cover.

THOMAS JEFFERSON

Mocking Bird, Houston, Texas

1

Branching the earthy lightness of his claws
upon a TV aerial, he unfolds
his borrowed repertoire, without applause
or varying the fragile clutch he holds
on multi-channelled masquerading choice;
he doesn't try to sell you fashioned things,
but runs his mocking through, voice after voice,
till, coming on his own again, unclings,
having fulfilled the present of his cause,
and crumples silence underneath his wings.

2

A bird we couldn't see
dropped song out of a tantalising tree,
not fashioning each individual note,
but imitating what it heard by rote.

Noting the copied sound,
we next day whistled at it from the ground;
but nothing answered. Tilting up to fly,
we saw it was a crow made no reply.

Could it be that birds find
a babel-language foreigning their kind
to baffle feathered signing, just as much
as we'd be, faced with Urdu or with Dutch?

MAURICE LINDSAY

The Bird of Paradise

When on a summer's morn I wake,
    And open my two eyes,
Out to the clear, born-singing rills,
    My bird-like spirit flies.

To hear the Blackbird, Cuckoo, Thrush,
    Or any bird in song;
And common leaves that hum all day,
    Without a throat or tongue.

And when Time strikes the hour for sleep,
    Back in my room alone,
My heart has many a sweet bird's song—
    And one that's all my own.

W H DAVIES

Coda

Other People's Flowers

Comme quelqu'un pourrait dire de moi que j'ai seulement fait ici un amas de fleurs étrangères, n'y ayant fourni du mien que le filet à les lier.

And one might therefore say of [us] that in this book [we] have only made up a bunch of other people's flowers, and that of [our] own [we] have only provided the string that ties them together.

M E MONTAIGNE

Envoi

In the name of the bee
And of the butterfly
And of the breeze
Amen.

EMILY DICKINSON

Glossary of Scots Words

abune above
abasit abashed
ane one
ase ash

band prison
bewis boughs
bontie bounty
bummers bees
buss bush

confortand comforting

doth me sike makes me sick
dreich persistently sad

for why because
fude food

garth garden

herberie greenery
het hot
hye haste

jenepere Juniper
jinkin moving in and out rapidly

kest cast
kirkyairdie-like such as grows in a
  churchyard

latting letting
lift sky
list pleased
louse loose

mells mixes
mo move

non offray no terror

pleyne disport

quhois whose
quhyte white
quite requite
quod said

silly poor
sudden abate sudden surprise
sue follow

tho a lite then a little while

weal riches
wenit held
whittern chirping
wote knows

ympis hymns
yorlin yellow hammer

Index of Authors and Sources